KNIT   READ   WALK

THE WEST
HIGHLAND
WAY

CONTENTS

DESIGNS

INFORMATION

The West Highland Way

I began with the colours of the landscape. I pictured a hat, knitted in the rich shades of autumn at Carbeth; a cardigan echoing the mossy hues of Conic Hill; a delicate jumper recalling a favourite plant found on Rannoch Moor. Each day, as I swatched and sketched and developed these designs, I opened my door to walk along my own patch of Scotland's most popular long-distance walking route, the West Highland Way. This is my locale: it's a landscape I know well, and I wanted to celebrate it in design.

As I worked, I thought more about this path, this landscape, and what I so loved about it. I walked through Glen Orchy and Glen Etive, Strathendrick and Strathfillan, Loch Lomondside and Lochaber. I thought about 2005, when I'd first walked here, a younger, different woman. I thought about what it meant to walk along the West Highland Way as the woman I am now. I thought about all the walking and thinking and making that had happened in this landscape, of the countless stories it had to tell. I found that my design work was further enriched by the history of the people who lived and worked here. The Craigallian fire-sitters. The Ben Nevis weathermen. The Blackwater navvies. The women who gathered the wool, spun the thread and waulked the cloth for a coat immortalised in song by Donnchadh Bàn. Soon I had a collection of designs, each of which had taken its beginning from the landscape, and through which a distinctive human story was also knitted.

Then I asked Tom (a photographer, and my husband) to join me on my creative journey. Our documentary impulses complement each other well: Tom creates images that inspire my words, and I write words that speak back to his images. Together, over several happy months, we walked and knitted and thought and saw and photographed and wrote our West Highland Way book into being. Tom spent a chilly moonlit night on Conic Hill, his camera taking a shot every 30 seconds.

He photographed the same famous local oak tree over the course of a whole year, depicting its self-sameness and its difference in all weathers, lights and seasonal changes. He hung out in bothies, sought out archaeological remains, stood in streams, fell in bogs, and climbed up a Stirling statue.

A SOCIAL LANDSCAPE

Everywhere Tom went, he saw people: people like us, who live and work here, in farming or forestry, textiles or tourism. And countless people too, who were there to enjoy the wonderful landscape of the West Highland Way: with their boots and rucksacks, taking a rest at the top of the Devil's Staircase, or jumping into the pools beneath the Falls of Falloch on a hot summer's day, relaxing in deck chairs by Loch Lomond's pebbled shores, drinking in the lovely view. Tom passed through the landscape, and he photographed it. And he also photographed me bimbling about the West Highland Way in the knitwear I'd designed.

With our work in design, writing and photography, Tom and I add our small something to the human story of our landscape. I find the social and cultural narrative of the West Highland Way just as compelling as its aesthetics. I hope that you do too, and that you enjoy the creative journey Tom and I have taken through these pages. And perhaps this book will inspire you to knit a hat or cardigan, or even to come here and join us walking along this wonderful long-distance route. To see something of our home, whose natural beauty is only matched by its cultural and historical riches. To take your own steps, your own photographs, develop your own memories, create your own stories. Perhaps you'll make your own West Highland Way. ☺☺

Designs and words by Kate Davies
Photography by Tom Barr

CRAIGALLIAN

These are the things that pull me
To the silent places and the windy places
And the places that are open and free.

Bob Grieve, *The Open Road*

It was a bright, warm June day when young Ian McHarg set off walking out of Glasgow with his friend Alistair McLean. Leaving the streets of their native city behind them, the boys tramped up the Stockiemuir and soon discovered what seemed to them another world: "bracken and heather underfoot ... wild strawberries grew on the stone walls. The path followed a burn almost continuously in waterfall, and in the pools were small trout and red-breasted minnows." Astounded by the beauty of the landscape, the boys dawdled over the muir until late afternoon before turning east along the narrow path which locals dubbed the Khyber Pass. Rising in and out of woodland, the boys finally spotted a narrow loch with an "encircling forest of beeches, mountain ash, and some pine and larch. Foxgloves and flag iris nodded along the margin, waterlilies colonised the water, dragonflies and damselfies flew." Behind the track that ran beside the loch, the boys came across a fire "with half a dozen people gathered about it", and sat down to join them in the dwindling evening light: "We listened enthralled to men who had travelled Scotland far and wide, picked grapes in France, and even more wondrous, had fought with the Scottish Brigade in the Spanish Civil War. They had light aluminium Bergen carriers, a Primus stove, a tin can and cup hanging from the pack, and big tackety boots." Like countless other young men walking out from Glasgow in the 1920s and 1930s, Ian and Alistair had made their way to the Craigallian Fire.

FIRE-SITTERS

These were the years of interwar depression. Among Glasgow's industrial communities, poverty was rife. While many unemployed men took to the hills, scraping together a living as itinerant, semi-tramping labourers, those who'd retained jobs joined their compatriots at the weekends, discovering in the landscapes on their doorstep a refreshing counterpoint to the stifling environments in which they laboured every day. Marking a convenient halfway point between city streets and northern hills, the woods by Craigallian Loch rapidly became a familiar gathering place, and the flames around which the working folk of Glasgow and Clydebank boiled their tea,

warmed their limbs and put the world to rights, before heading north into the hills, soon became known as "the fire that never went out". "Coming along the track of a winter's evening," Matt Forrester recalled, "the glow of light and the merry shouts of laughter brought joy to the heart. One could always be assured of company there, good company, and pleasant tales of the countryside."

To the light, warmth and welcome of the Craigallian Fire can be traced the informal beginnings of the Scottish outdoor movement. The Ptarmigan Mountaineering Club was founded beside the Craigallian Fire by Jock Nimlin and his friends. A Clydeside crane operative, Jock was notorious among his fellow fire-sitters for never having missed a weekend out of doors for over five years. He later worked with the National Trust for Scotland, developing a new network of rural rangers. Bob Grieve, who had first sat by the Craigallian Fire as an unemployed apprentice, trained as a civil engineer and later went on to play a leading role in Scotland's environmental and rural affairs as the first chair of the Highlands and Islands Development Board and president of the Scottish Mountaineering Council. Chris Lyon, who found his way to the fire as a teenage worker in the Clydebank Singer sewing-machine factory, became president of the Creagh Dhu mountaineering club and a talented and vocal advocate of Scotland's outdoor movement. Chris recalls that politics continually dominated the discourse of the older men who inspired him around the Craigallian Fire. "They spoke a new language," he recalled: "dialectical materialism." Young Ian McHarg was similarly powerfully struck by the political and philosophical nature of Craigallian conversation. "I discovered that these men spent much time during inclement winters in public libraries."

While fewer women than men found their way to the flames of the Craigallian Fire, the surrounding area became a focal point for the activities of socialist women too. In 1918, the land around Carbeth had been dedicated by a progressive local landowner to the leisure of local working people. Among the outdoor and political organisations to find their roots here was the Fellowship Camping Association, who took for their motto Rose Schneiderman's words about working-class dignity: "the worker must have bread, but she must have roses too". Every weekend, the working women of Glasgow and Clydebank gathered at the FCA camp to enjoy the roses of Carbeth and Craigallian: swimming at the purpose-built lido, sharing their ideas and

creativity in art and reading groups, and participating in outdoor ante-natal classes (revolutionary, for their time). Notable women activists, such as Glasgow labour campaigner Bunty Urquhart, spent their childhood weekends at Carbeth, and many young women discovered here a love of their local landscape and of walking that was to last a lifetime. Bearsden hillwalker, Margaret Cadenhead, traces her enduring love of the great Scottish outdoors back to the weekends she spent as a child in the 1930s, enjoying the warmth and conviviality of the Craigallian Fire.

"THE EVERYDAY USE OF THE GREAT OUTDOORS"

And what of young Ian McHarg, who first found his way to Craigallian Loch on that fine June day? Ian's love of his local landscape never left him, and nor did the environmental and philosophical lessons he learned beside the fire. He went on to become a renowned academic and urban planner in the USA, much admired for his pioneering work with sustainable and regenerative design. Highlighting the profound effects of outdoor spaces on the human psyche, his 1969 book *Design with Nature* was a game-changer in its field.

"The people who passed through this spot in the 1930s were unknowingly starting something which would be taken for granted by future generations," recalls Scott Valentine: "the everyday use of the great outdoors by the ordinary person." Today, thousands of ordinary people, from all over the world, pass the location of the Craigallian Fire as they begin their journey north, into the hills, along the West Highland Way.

After walking through Mugdock Country Park, your path rises beside Craigallian Loch, and if you look to your left a few hundred yards beyond the water, you'll see the location of the fire. There's a sheltered spot under the trees, a bracken-covered slope rising up behind, and a burn that flows merrily down the hill. You'll also see the modest memorial, designed by sculptor Tim Chalk, and placed here in 2012 to commemorate the fire. Why not take a seat by the memorial, open a flask of tea, read the words inscribed into the stone, and pause to remember those who gathered together here in the last century's early decades? To these revolutionary talkers and walkers, to these working-class pedestrian pioneers, we owe the basic principles of open access and the roots of the outdoor movement which has opened up Scotland's landscape for the enjoyment of so many people today. And, as you rise to your feet to continue your walk along the West Highland Way, you'll be following in the footsteps of Craigallian's inspiring fire-sitters. ◎◎

HERE BURNED THE CRAIGALLIAN FIRE DURING THE DEPRESSION OF THE 1930s. AS A BEACON OF COMPANIONSHIP AND HOPE FOR YOUNG UNEMPLOYED PEOPLE WHO CAME FROM GLASGOW AND CLYDEBANK SEEKING ADVENTURE IN SCOTLAND'S WILD PLACES. THEIR PIONEERING SPIRIT HELPED TO MAKE THE SCOTTISH COUNTRYSIDE FREE FOR ALL TO ROAM

CRAIGALLIAN HAT

A cosy beanie, combining colour and texture, in four seasonal colourways.

YARN
Kate Davies Designs Milarrochy Tweed (70% Wool; 30% Mohair; 100m / 109yds per 25g ball)

Spring
A: Birkin
B: Garth
C: Hirst
D: Smirr
E: Stockiemuir

Summer
A: Garth
B: Hirst
C: Stockiemuir
D: Campion
E: Ardlui

Autumn
A: Horseback brown
B: Birkin
C: Buckthorn
D: Garth
E: Gloamin'

Winter
A: Smirr
B: Lochan
C: Bruce
D: Ardlui
E: Hirst

Sample hats knit at the specified gauge used the following approximate yarn quantities – be aware that small differences in gauge will affect yarn usage:

A: 13g
B: 14g
C: 5g
D: 8g
E: 7g

NEEDLES AND NOTIONS
Below gauge-size circular needle, 40cm / 16in length for rib
Gauge-size circular needle, 40cm / 16in length for main body.
Gauge-size needle(s) of your preferred type for working crown shaping.
Stitch marker.
Tapestry needle.

GAUGE
28 sts and 36 rounds to 10cm / 4in over stranded colourwork pattern using gauge-size needle.
Gauge was achieved with 3.25mm / US 3 needle.

SIZE
One size to fit head circumference: 51-56cm / 20-22in
Hat circumference (unstretched): 52.5cm / 20½in
Height from brim to crown: 21cm / 8¼in
Depending on your preference, this hat can be stretched and blocked to create a relatively slouchy shape or blocked into a neatly-fitting beanie.

PATTERN NOTES
This hat is knitted in the round from the bottom up, following a colourwork chart. Charts appear on following two pages, hat instructions begin on page 14.

CHART NOTES
Read each row of the chart from right to left throughout.

ABBREVIATIONS
Standard abbreviations appear on the inside back cover.

CRAIGALLIAN HAT

KEY

- ■ k in shade indicated
- ◉ p in shade indicated
- ⩕ cdd in shade indicated

SPRING

- A: Birkin, k
- B: Garth, k
- C: Hirst, k
- D: Smirr, k
- E: Stockiemuir, k

SUMMER

- A: Garth, k
- B: Hirst, k
- C: Stockiemuir, k
- D: Campion, k
- E: Ardlui, k

CHART: SPRING COLOURWAY

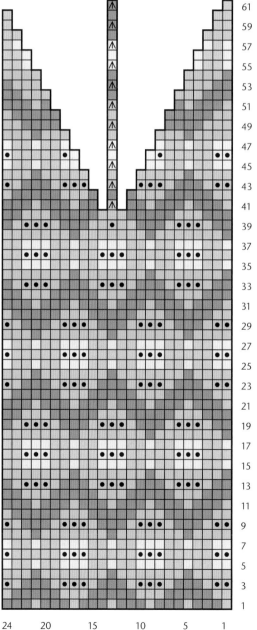

CHART: SUMMER COLOURWAY

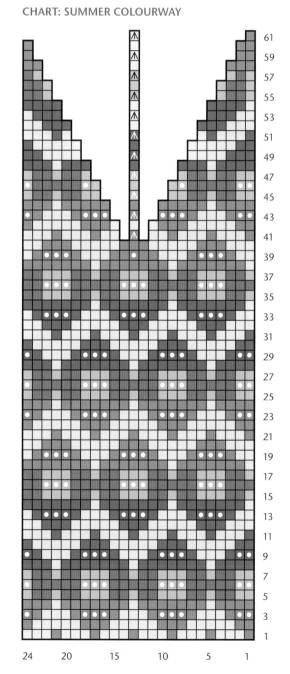

CRAIGALLIAN HAT

KEY

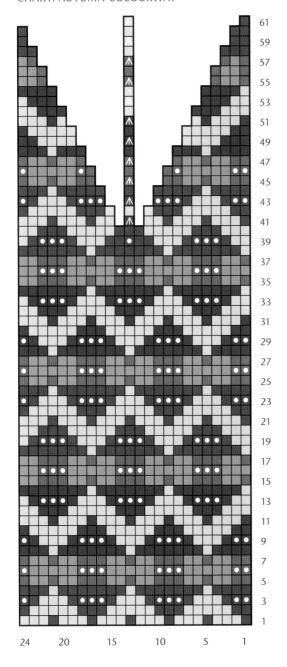

- ▨ k in shade indicated
- ⬡ p in shade indicated
- ⋀ cdd in shade indicated

AUTUMN

- ▨ A: Horseback brown, k
- ☐ B: Birkin, k
- ▨ C: Buckthorn, k
- ▨ D: Garth, k
- ▨ E: Gloamin', k

WINTER

- ☐ A: Smirr, k
- ▨ B: Lochan, k
- ▨ C: Bruce, k
- ▨ D: Ardlui, k
- ☐ E: Hirst, k

CHART: AUTUMN COLOURWAY

CHART: WINTER COLOURWAY

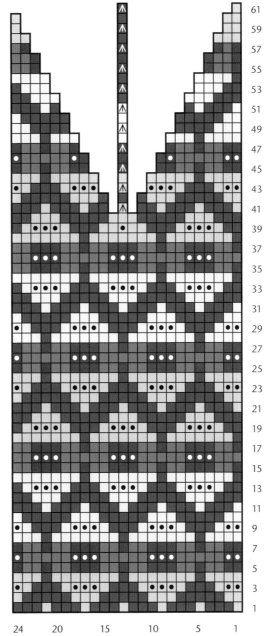

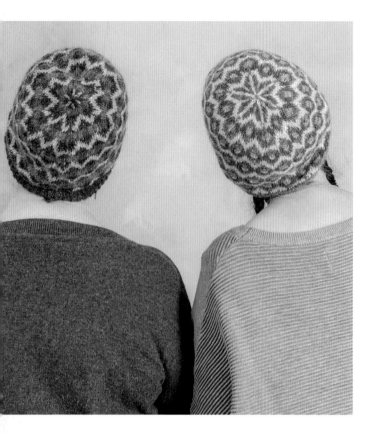

HAT INSTRUCTIONS

1

WORK BRIM

With shade C and 40cm / 16in below gauge-size circular needle, cast on 120 sts, pm, and join for working in the round.
Break off C and join in A.
Round 1: *P1, k1tbl; rep from * to end.
Last round sets 1x1 twisted rib.
Rep last round a further 11 times.

2

MAIN BODY AND CHART

Change to 40cm / 16in gauge-size circular needle.
Increase round: *K5, m1; rep from * to end. *24 sts inc; 144 sts.*
Commence working from chart as foll:
Changing shades, working purl sts and decreases where indicated, and repeating chart 6 times across each round, work chart rounds 1-61 changing to gauge-size needle(s) of your preferred type for working crown shaping as st count decreases. *132 sts dec; 12 sts rem.*

Next round: With A, (k2tog) 6 times. *6 sts dec; 6 sts rem.*
Break yarn, thread through remaining sts, draw yarn down through the centre of the gathered sts and fasten off to inside of crown.

3

FINISHING

Weave in all ends to the back of the work. Soak hat in cool water for 20-30 minutes to allow sts to relax, then remove water by pressing between dry towels. Block hat to dimensions given over hat block, or foam head, or using plastic bags to shape, taking care not to stretch rib out of shape – a length of sock yarn may be threaded and tightened around brim and drawn together during the blocking process to prevent rib from over stretching.

Enjoy your Craigallian hat!

CRAIGALLIAN MITTS AND MITTENS

Graphic mitts or mittens featuring the Craigallian pattern and afterthought thumbs.

YARN
Kate Davies Designs Milarrochy Tweed (70% Wool; 30% Mohair; 100m / 109yds per 25g ball)
A: Birkin; 1 x 25g ball
B: Buckthorn; 1 x 25g ball
C: Smirr; 1 x 25g ball
D: Horseback brown; 1 x 25g ball
E: Bruce; 1 x 25g ball

Sample mitts/mittens knit at the specified gauge used the following approximate yarn quantities – be aware that small differences in gauge will affect yarn usage:

Mitts	Mittens
A: 8g	**A:** 12.5g
B: 6.5g	**B:** 8.5g
C: 4g	**C:** 6g
D: 4g	**D:** 6g
E: 11.5g	**E:** 16.5g

NEEDLES AND NOTIONS
Gauge-size and below gauge-size needle(s) of your preferred type for working small circumferences.
Waste yarn (for thumb placement).
Stitch marker.
Tapestry needle.

GAUGE
34 sts and 38 rounds to 10cm / 4in over stranded colourwork pattern using gauge-size needle.
Gauge was achieved with 3mm / US 2½ needle.

SIZE
Hand circumference above thumb: 19cm / 7½in
Length of mitts from cuff to top: 16.5cm / 6½in
Length of mittens from cuff to top: 23cm / 9¼in

SPECIAL TECHNIQUES
Grafting (Kitchener Stitch) – see Special Techniques section on page 126.

PATTERN NOTES
The mitts (or mittens) are cast on, and a cuff worked in twisted rib. After increasing stitches and beginning to work from the colourwork chart, a placeholder of waste yarn is inserted into the fabric of the palm for the afterthought thumb. The chart is completed, then the mitts finished with an open rib, or a closed, grafted top for the mittens. The waste yarn placeholder is then removed, and the afterthought thumb completed.

CHART NOTES
Read each row of the chart from right to left throughout.

ABBREVIATIONS
Standard abbreviations appear on the inside back cover.

MITT INSTRUCTIONS

1

CAST ON, WORK CUFF

With shade B and below gauge-size needle(s), cast on 52 sts, pm, and join for working in the round. Break off B and join in E.
Round 1: *P1, k1tbl; rep from * to end.
Last round sets 1x1 twisted rib.
Rep last round a further 19 times.

2

WORK HAND

Change to gauge-size needle(s).
Increase round: (K4, m1) 12 times, k4. *12 sts inc; 64 sts.*
Commence working from chart as foll:
Changing shades, working purl sts where indicated, and repeating chart twice across each round, work chart rounds 1-23.

3

THUMB PLACEMENT, COMPLETE CHART

Next round: Working chart round 24, insert thumb placeholder as foll; with A k1, then, with waste yarn, k9, return these 9 sts to LH needle and continue working chart round 24 as est.
Afterthought thumb marker now placed across 9 waste-yarn sts.
Continue working chart rounds 25-41.

4

MITT TOP

Change to below gauge-size needle(s) and continue with E only.
Decrease round: K4, (k2tog, k3) 12 times. *12 sts dec; 52 sts rem.*
Work 1x1 twisted rib as for cuff for 8 rounds.
With B, bind off in pattern.

5

THUMB

With below gauge-size needle(s) and E, puk right legs of the 9 sts under row of waste yarn, turn mitt 180 degrees and puk 9 sts above the waste yarn in the same way. *18 sts.*
Carefully remove the waste yarn.
Round 1: *K9, puk 1 st in gap between needles; rep from * once more, pm. *2 sts inc; 20 sts.*
Work 1x1 twisted rib as for cuff for 6 rounds.
With B, bind off in rib.

6

SECOND MITT

Follow steps 1-5 to make a second mitt in exactly the same way.

7

FINISHING

Weave in all ends to the back of the work, paying particular attention to the thumb join, which may need neatening. Soak mitts in cool water for 20 mins and press between towels to remove water. Shape mitts and block over a pair of glove blockers (if you have them), or pin out to finished dimensions, designating one mitt left and other mitt right. Dry flat and allow to fully dry.

Enjoy your Craigallian mitts!

MITTEN INSTRUCTIONS

Repeating chart twice across each round, work steps 1 and 2 exactly as for mitts above.

3a

RIGHT THUMB PLACEMENT

Next round: Working chart round 24, insert thumb placeholder as foll; with A k1, then, with waste yarn, k9, return these 9 sts to LH needle and continue working chart round 24 as est.
Afterthought thumb marker now placed across 9 waste-yarn sts.

3b

LEFT THUMB PLACEMENT

Next round: Working chart round 24, insert thumb placeholder as foll; changing shades as indicated k22 from chart round 24, then, with waste yarn, k9, return these 9 sts to LH needle and complete chart round 24 as est. *Afterthought thumb marker now placed across 9 waste-yarn sts.*

4

COMPLETE CHART, GRAFT TOP

Changing shades and working decreases where indicated, work chart rounds 25-71. *20 sts rem.*
With E, graft together 2 sets of 10 sts at mitten top.

5 THUMB

With below-gauge needle(s) and E, puk right legs of the 9 sts under row of waste yarn, turn mitt 180 degrees and puk 9 sts above the waste yarn in the same way. *18 sts.*
Carefully remove the waste yarn.
Round 1: *K9, puk 1 st in gap between needles; rep from * once more, pm. *2 sts inc; 20 sts.*
Redistribute sts on needle(s) as preferred.
Change to gauge-size needle(s), and with A, k until thumb is 1cm / 2/5in shorter than desired length (22 rounds will give an average thumb length).
Next round: (K2tog) 10 times. *10 sts dec; 10 sts rem.*
Knit 2 rounds.
Next round: (K2tog) 5 times. *5 sts dec; 5 sts rem.*
Break yarn and draw up tightly through remaining 5 sts.
Fasten off to inside of thumb.

6 WORK ANOTHER MITTEN

Following relevant right or left thumb instructions.

7 FINISHING

Weave in all ends to the back of the work, paying particular attention to the thumb join, which may need neatening. Soak mittens in cool water for 20 minutes and press between towels to remove water. Shape mitts and block over a pair of glove blockers (if you have them), or pin out to finished dimensions. Dry flat and allow to fully dry.

Enjoy your Craigallian mittens!

KEY

A: Birkin, k
B: Buckthorn, k
C: Smirr, k
D: Horseback brown, k
E: Bruce, k
p in shade indicated
ssk in shade indicated
k2tog in shade indicated
round 41 – end for mitt
24 round 24 – insert thumb

CHART

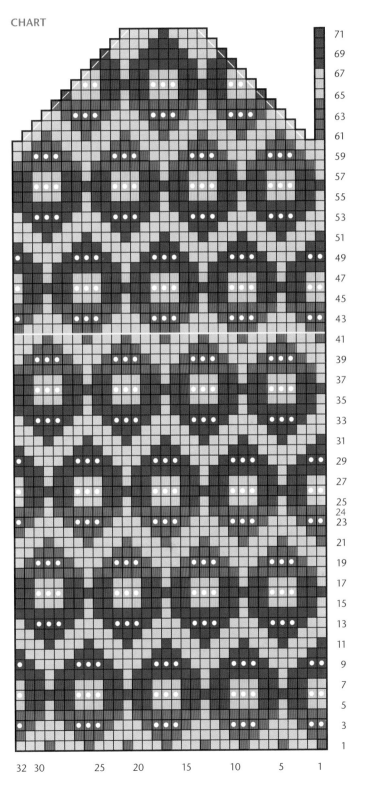

STRATHENDRICK

We are mere transients who sing
Its westlin winds and fernie braes.

Kathleen Jamie, *Here Lies our Land*

I put on my hat, close the door behind me, and walk out into the air. I hear the soft whoosh of two swans overhead and raise my hand to greet them. I know this old pair very well: they nest by the loch behind my house, and, like me, they are creatures of habit, rising daily in the early morning light to complete a circuit of their neighbourhood.

The gate where I join the West Highland Way opens and closes with its familiar creaking sound. On old maps, this part of the way goes by the name *Tinker's Loan*. The smooth stones beneath my feet, the crumbling walls at the field margin, the immediate sense of this path as a well-worn passageway from here to there – all call to mind the countless other people who have traversed this landscape. Other feet, and other walkers. Tinkers selling ribbons, mending tools, seeking seasonal labour; drovers calling cattle from the hills, moving them onwards, eastwards to the tryst. Passing through, sometimes abiding, making their living here.

ACROSS THE SKYLINE

After a short rise, another gate and another dry stone wall, the landscape opens out. The volcanic crags of Dumgoyne rise up, and beside them the terraces of the Campsie Fells stretch away. Yet it is the view north-west that really draws the eye. This is where many travellers, a few miles into the West Highland Way, first stop, gaze out and think "ah, *that* is where I'm going". The strath stretches low, broad and wide, away to the shores of Loch Lomond, and above it the western hills call the walker onwards. In the distance, you can make out Ben Ìme, Ben Vane, Ben Vorlich and the Cobbler's distinctive crescent summit, but it is the great hump of Ben Lomond that dominates the skyline, stretched out above the loch like a huge animal in sleep. Scan the horizon and just a few miles ahead you'll see the cheery, knobbly ridge of Conic Hill, whose heather-clad slopes you will soon encounter as you walk on. This view never looks the same, and it always fills the heart. Like those seeing the Highlands before them for the very first time, I pause, breathe, and drink the landscape in.

Now, will you walk with me down the strath?

Strath is the word in Scotland for a wide river valley, and on my daily walks along the West Highland Way I traverse two such: Strathendrick and Strathblane. Cutting their broad paths through the rocky landscape, these scoured-out valleys were first formed by slowly moving ice, and the ground beneath my feet is made up of glacial moraine. The strath's floor is low and undulating, but there's a sharp descent to reach it. I gather my wits, prepare my leg. Like other disabled walkers, my relationship with surfaces and inclines is perhaps more than ordinarily attentive. I assess the implications of each slope and each rise, and often have to think about the very substance of the strath. I reflect on the differences of rubble and silt, peat and shingle, consider the dramatic effects of rain and gales or how repeated freeze–thaws might transform the stable ground into a sponge. Small environmental changes can dramatically affect my body's abilities and resources. Yet the benefit of years of such forced attention is that I now understand this strath so very closely that I could walk here in the dark. I sometimes do.

THE LANDSCAPE'S HUMAN STORY

In this landscape, there is always life. Darting in front of me on my early-morning walks are hares, weasels and the ubiquitous red deer with whom I compete for possession of my vegetable garden. The grassy margins of the strath play host to reed buntings, skylarks and curlews, while ravens nest high in the crags above. Between April and June, the wooded slopes of Dumgoyach ring out with cuckoos' calls, while hen harriers, owl-faced and elegant, patrol a landscape criss-crossed with voles. Beside the burns, newts make their homes, and throughout the year the strath is a tapestry of continually changing floral colour. Yellow tormentil sits against blue-white eyebright, while ragged robin, foxglove and water avens tussle to attain the most delicious shade of pink. For a few wondrous weeks, north-facing hollows have an unearthly bluebell glow, and the brown boggy ground upon which nobody treads transforms itself into a magic carpet of wild orchids, all shimmering shades of mauve. The flora-rich muir is beautiful but unremunerative, and the current landowners have recently decided to change things with extensive formal planting. I walk here and wonder how the forestry and deer-fencing will transform the strath – but the coming conifers are just one page in the long story of this landscape.

It is, of course, a familiar story, a human story, a story of how to make use of the land. If we turn to look back towards Dumgoyne here, you'll see a row of megaliths, some recumbent now, on the flat, raised plain beyond. Neolithic humans were walking here between 2800 and 270 BC, and the stones they left mark what is likely to have been a long chambered tomb. Behind the standing stones, the Duntreath estate still dominates the landscape, as it has done in its various forms since the fifteenth century.

Dotted along the strath, you'll find a few small, ancient farm steadings (some recently renovated and rebuilt, like my own home), while the boundary lines that appear in nineteenth-century mapping point to particular narratives of exclusion and enclosure. The river once provided water for the distillery which we are now passing on our right, while local names like *Stockiemuir* recall a long history of common pasture. Perhaps a good way to understand this landscape, then, is as a place of continual passage, for the strath has always been a route, a road, for humans and other creatures.

Leaving the rugged muir behind, the path suddenly straightens out. For the firm, even ground beneath our feet, we can thank those who constructed the Blane Valley railway line (opened in 1861, and closed in 1959). In one direction, the trains carried milk and other rural produce along the strath to Glasgow, and in the other direction they brought visitors north to see the beauty of the Trossachs, Loch Lomond and Loch Katrine. The steam trains are long gone, but the visitors are still coming, travelling by car or coach, or moving steadily on foot, like us, along the old track that is now the West Highland Way.

Strathendrick and Strathblane. Valleys filled with life and moving feet. Places of passage, liminal places, spaces of anticipation before the drama of the hills. Every year, thousands of people walking the West Highland Way travel down these straths like you and I. On a warm afternoon, the place can have a party atmosphere, the air ringing out with the sounds of many different languages. People from all over the world come here to see a little of Scotland, to enjoy their own Highland adventure. On summer evenings, I open my door to visitors from Germany, Portugal, the USA. I fill their bottles with water, lend them a box of matches, show them the best place to camp out on the muir. Young and old, from as nearby as Duntocher or as far away as New Zealand, it makes me glad to see these walkers stepping westwards through the landscape where neolithic settlers, early-modern drovers and Victorian tinkers have all stepped before. Come all ye. All are welcome here. Strathblane and Strathendrick. I walk here, I abide here; here I make my living. But, like you, and like every other traveller whose feet have moved down this strath, down the centuries, I am simply passing through. ☉☉

STRATHENDRICK

A statement allover sweater in which a contemporary oversized look combines with a vintage Fairisle feel.

YARN

Kate Davies Designs Milarrochy Tweed (70% Wool; 30% Mohair; 100m / 109yds per 25g ball)
A: Hirst; 9 (10, 10, 11) x 25g balls
B: Ardlui; 2 (2, 2, 2) x 25g balls
C: Lochan; 5 (5, 6, 6) x 25g balls
D: Garth; 2 (3, 3, 3) x 25g balls
E: Campion; 2 (2, 2, 2) x 25g balls
F: Stockiemuir; 1 (1, 1, 1) x 25g balls

NEEDLES AND NOTIONS

Gauge-size and below gauge-size circular needles of appropriate length for working body.
Below gauge-size circular needle of appropriate length for working neckband.
Gauge-size and below gauge-size needle(s) of your preferred type for working small circumferences.
6 stitch markers.
Waste yarn for provisional cast on and reinforcing steeks.
Optional: ribbon or bias tape for finishing steek edges

GAUGE

28 sts and 36 rounds to 10cm / 4in over colourwork pattern **and** stockinette in the round using gauge-size needle.
Gauge was achieved with 3.25mm / US 3 needle.

SIZES

Finished bust circumference: 164 (174, 184, 194) cm / 64 (68, 72, 76) in
Sweater should be worn with 51-81cm / 20-32in positive ease
Shown in the first size with 81cm / 32in positive ease at bust

SIZING TABLE

	1st	2nd	3rd	4th	
HIP CIRCUMFERENCE (ROUNDED TO NEAREST CM/IN)					
	150	163	170	183	cm
	59	64	67	72	in
LENGTH FROM HEM TO UNDERARM					
	42.5	42.5	44	44	cm
	16¾	16¾	17¼	17¼	in
BUST CIRCUMFERENCE					
	164	174	184	194	cm
	64	68	72	76	in
TOTAL LENGTH					
	64	65	66.5	67.5	cm
	25¼	25½	26¼	26½	in
SHOULDER					
	29	31.5	33.5	36	cm
	11½	12½	13¼	14¼	in
NECK CIRCUMFERENCE					
	47	47	48.5	48.5	cm
	18½	18½	19	19	in
ARM CIRCUMFERENCE AT ELBOW / SLEEVE JOIN					
	25.5	27	27.5	29	cm
	10	10½	11	11½	in
CUFF					
	17.5	17.5	19	19	cm
	7	7	7½	7½	in
SLEEVE TO JOIN					
	25.5	27	27.5	29	cm
	10	10½	11	11½	in

SCHEMATIC

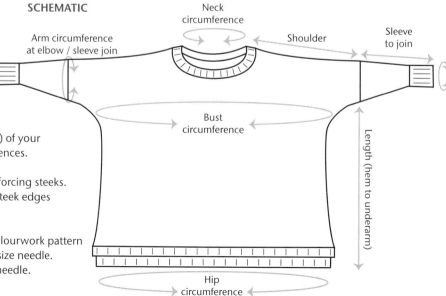

SPECIAL TECHNIQUES

Steeks; Two-colour grafting; Picking up stitches adjacent to a steek; Provisional cast on – see Special Techniques section on page 126.

Keeping pattern correct in colourwork

When shaping is worked close to the underarms, you'll need to treat front and back as two separate pieces in order to "keep the pattern correct" within the shaping. This may sound tricky, but by the time you've reached this point on your sweater, the rhythm of the pattern is likely to feel intuitive. You may find it helpful to print off / copy another chart repeat, drawing the lines of increased stitches directly onto the chart, and to use extra stitch markers to separate the new repeat.
thisisknit.ie/shaping-in-lace/

Working shaping in pattern

On the neckline, you'll note that the shaping slants toward the steek lines (the opposite way to which you may be used to working such decreases). This shift in direction ensures that any disruption to the pattern is minimised.

PATTERN NOTES

The sweater is cast on provisionally and worked in the round to just below the underarms, where sleeve shaping is worked outward. Armscye steeks are added, followed by another steek to create the neckline shaping, and the sweater body is worked up to the shoulders, whose stitches are then grafted. After cutting the armscye steeks, sleeves are worked from the top down, and ribbing worked around the neckline after cutting the final steek. The sweater is finished by adding ribbing for front and back hems separately. Where only one number is given this applies to all sizes.

CHART NOTES

Read each row of the chart from right to left throughout.

ABBREVIATIONS

Standard abbreviations appear on the inside back cover.

INSTRUCTIONS

1

CAST ON, WORK BODY

With long circular gauge-size needle and waste yarn, provisionally cast on 414 (450, 468, 504) sts, pm, and join for working in the round.
Join in shades A and B and begin working from chart round 1, placing a second marker after 207 (225, 234, 252) sts and repeating the chart 23 (25, 26, 28) times across the round.
Continue working from chart, repeating as necessary and changing shades as indicated, until piece from cast-on edge measures 37 (38, 38, 39.5) cm / 14½ (15, 15, 15½) in.

2

SIDE INCREASES

Next round: Keeping pattern correct, increase as foll:
X: *K1, m1, k to 1 st before marker, m1, k1, slm; rep from * once more. *4 sts inc.*
Y: Work 1 round.
Rep steps X and Y a further 8 (6, 8, 6) times. *36 (28, 36, 28) sts inc; 450 (478, 504, 532) sts.*

Work final increases as foll to ensure the pattern is mirrored, front and back, and will match at the shoulders:
For all sizes: * K to 1 st before marker, m1, k1, slm; rep from * once more. *2 sts inc; 452 (480, 506, 534) sts total; 226 (240, 253, 267) sts each front and back.*
Next round: Work to end.

3

ARMSCYE STEEKS

Insert steek sts to shape armscye openings as foll:
Next round: Keeping pattern correct, *using backwards loop method and alternating working yarns, cast on 9 sts, pm, k to marker, slm; rep from * once more. *18 steek sts cast on for armscyes.*
Keeping pattern for front and back correct as est, working steek sts in alternating shades throughout, work until piece measures 9 (9.5, 10, 11) cm / 3½ (3¾, 4, 4¼) in from start of steek.

4

NECK STEEK, NECK SHAPING

Insert steek sts to shape neck opening as foll:
Next round: Work 9 steek sts, slm, k88 (95, 100, 107) of front, pm, sl next 50 (50, 53, 53) sts to waste yarn, using backwards loop method and alternating working yarns cast on 9 steek sts, pm, k88 (95, 100, 107) front sts, slm, k9 steek sts, slm, k226 (240, 253, 267) back sts. *Front neck steek sts are now set up between markers.*

Commence neck shaping as foll:
Next round (dec): Work 9 arm steek sts, slm, k across front to 2 sts before marker, ssk, slm, k9 neck steek sts, slm, k2tog, work to end of round keeping pattern and steek sts correct. *2 sts dec.*
Rep last round a further 7 times. *16 sts dec; 436 (464, 490, 518) sts rem.*
Keeping pattern and steek sts correct, work until piece measures 14 (14.5, 15, 16) cm / 5½ (5¾, 6, 6¼) in from start of arm steek.

CHART

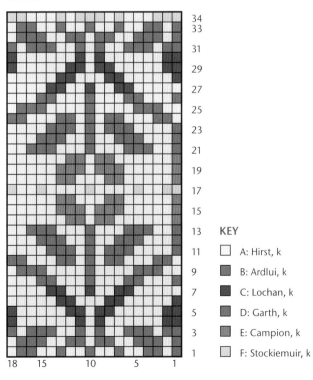

34	
33	
31	
29	
27	
25	
23	
21	
19	
17	
15	
13	**KEY**
11	☐ A: Hirst, k
9	▦ B: Ardlui, k
7	■ C: Lochan, k
5	▦ D: Garth, k
3	▨ E: Campion, k
1	▤ F: Stockiemuir, k

18   15   10   5   1

5

BIND OFF STEEKS, GRAFT SHOULDERS

Keeping pattern correct, removing all markers as you encounter them, work as foll:

Next round: Bind off 9 armscye steek sts, k to marker, bind off 9 neck steek sts, k to marker, bind off 9 armscye steek sts, k146 (153, 161, 168) sts, sl 66 (66, 69, 69) sts just worked to waste yarn, k80 (87, 92, 99) sts to end. *Back neck is now set aside on waste yarn and 2 sets of 80 (87, 92, 99) back shoulder sts rem live on needle.*

Sl 2 sets of 80 (87, 92, 99) front shoulder sts to a second needle and, with A plus your relevant contrast shade, graft front right and back right, and then front left and back left shoulder sts together in pattern (joining like shade to like). *Refer to the tutorial linked in special techniques.*

6

SLEEVES

Reinforce and cut sleeve steeks (referring to special techniques).

With RS facing, C and gauge-size needle(s) of your preferred type for working small circumferences, beginning at centre point of underarm, puk 35 (37, 38, 40) sts up sleeve to shoulder, puk 35 (37, 38, 40) sts down sleeve to underarm, pm. *70 (74, 76, 80) sts*

Next round: Working with C in plain stockinette throughout, begin sleeve shaping as foll:

X: Slm, k1, k2tog, work to 3 sts before end of round, ssk, k1. *2 sts dec.*

Y: Work 4 rounds.

Rep steps X and Y a further 10 (12, 11, 13) times. *22 (26, 24, 28) sts dec; 48 (48, 52, 52) sts rem.*

Work further rounds (if required) until sleeve from join measures 18 (19, 20.5, 21.5) cm / 7 (7½, 8, 8½) in.

Change to below gauge-size needle.

Next round: *K1tbl, p1; rep from * to end.

Last round sets 1x1 twisted rib.

Rep last round until cuff measures 7.5cm / 3in, or desired length to wrist.

Bind off in rib.

Make another sleeve in the same way.

7

NECKBAND

Reinforce and cut neck steek (referring to special techniques).

Sl 66 (66, 69, 69) held back neck sts to smaller, below gauge-size needle. Working from right back shoulder, sl first 33 (33, 34, 34) sts, pm for new start of round, rejoin working yarn, k33 (33, 35, 35) sts, puk 12 sts down left front neck, sl 50 (50, 53, 53) sts from centre front neck to spare needle and k across them, puk 12 sts up right front neck, k33 (33, 34, 34) back neck sts. *140 (140, 146, 146) sts.*

Working in 1x1 twisted rib throughout (as est for cuff), dec 10 (10, 12, 12) sts evenly across first round. *130 (130, 134, 134) sts.*

Work in 1x1 twisted rib until neckband measures 5cm / 2in.

Bind off in rib.

8

HEM

Unzip provisional cast-on and place 207 (225, 235, 253) back sts on below gauge-size needle leaving rem sts on hold for now. Join in C.

Row 1 (RS): *K1tbl, p1; rep from * to last st, k1tbl.

Row 2 (WS): *P1tbl, k1; rep from * to to last st, p1tbl.

Last 2 rows set 1x1 twisted rib.

Work in 1x1 twisted rib for 7.5cm / 3in ending with a WS row

Bind off in rib.

Return to sts held for front, and sl 207 (225, 233, 251) sts from waste yarn to below gauge-size needle. Join in C and work in 1x1 twisted rib as est for back, for 2.5cm / 1in.

Bind off in rib.

9

FINISHING

Weave in all ends to the back of the work. Trim steeks (if required) and carefully stitch down to WS of fabric, covering raw edges with a ribbon / facing (if preferred). Soak sweater in cool water for 20-30mins, press out water between dry towels, pin out flat to dimensions in sizing table, carefully stretching and adjusting shoulders to form a slight slope from neckline to elbow, and leave to fully dry.

Enjoy your Strathendrick sweater!

CÒINNEACH

Crags, knolls and mounds, confusedly hurled
The fragments of an earlier world.

Walter Scott, *The Lady of the Lake*

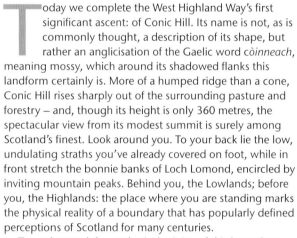

Today we complete the West Highland Way's first significant ascent: of Conic Hill. Its name is not, as is commonly thought, a description of its shape, but rather an anglicisation of the Gaelic word *còinneach*, meaning mossy, which around its shadowed flanks this landform certainly is. More of a humped ridge than a cone, Conic Hill rises sharply out of the surrounding pasture and forestry – and, though its height is only 360 metres, the spectacular view from its modest summit is surely among Scotland's finest. Look around you. To your back lie the low, undulating straths you've already covered on foot, while in front stretch the bonnie banks of Loch Lomond, encircled by inviting mountain peaks. Behind you, the Lowlands; before you, the Highlands: the place where you are standing marks the physical reality of a boundary that has popularly defined perceptions of Scotland for many centuries.

To understand the geological origins of this boundary, turn south-west and trace a path with your eye down the ridge of the hill across the glassy surface of the loch. You'll see the islands of Inchcailloch, Torrinch, Creinch and Inchmurrin dotted along the water in a clearly visible line – and, if the day is clear, your eye might continue to follow this trajectory all the way to the west coast and the Isle of Bute.

Here, cutting across Conic Hill and Loch Lomond, is the Highland Boundary Fault. The fault is more than 140 miles long and effectively divides Scotland in two: gently rolling lowland on one side, and rough highland terrain on the other. Some 520 to 400 million years ago, ancient continental fragments collided with each other along the fault line during the closure of the Iapetus Ocean. The harder highland rocks were raised and uplifted, while the softer lowland sediments sank down into deep valleys. To the north and west of the boundary fault zone are the silvery schists and gneisses of the Dalradian group, while to the south and east lie softer Devonian and Carboniferous rocks such as Old Red Sandstone. Walking the West Highland Way from Conic Hill along Loch Lomond's

eastern shoreline is also a fascinating journey across fault-zone geology. Beneath your feet at Balmaha, the cobbles of sedimentary conglomerate gradually give way to breccias and serpentines around Milarrochy Bay – and, by the time you reach Rowardennan, the bedrock has become a silvery, folded Highland schist, whose visible scars tell the story of the glacier which formed Loch Lomond long ago.

Land and water have an important relationship here, and to understand the nature of their coexistence you might change your method of transport from foot to vessel. Though the free-to-use canoes moored at the lochside by the infamous Creagh Dhu mountaineering club (named "May Day" and "Revolution") are no longer there, you can still nip out on a paddle board, hire a kayak at Balmaha boatyard, join the regular local sailings to picnic on Inchcailloch, or take a short cruise with one of the many companies operating around Loch Lomond's western shores. There are over fifty islands in Loch Lomond (though definitions of "island" tend to vary), and archaeological studies have revealed that humans were living on and around these waters as early as 5000 BC. On the beautiful island of Inchlonaig, tools and other Stone Age artefacts point to the fact that settlers came here long before Robert the Bruce planted his fabled groves of yews, dedicating the trees to be used in bow-making.

ISLAND CONNECTIONS

Many of Loch Lomond's smaller islands are not, in fact, "real" islands at all, but rather crannogs: artificial structures used between the late Bronze Age and the seventeenth century that have, over time, assumed the appearance of small islets. One example is Inchgalbraith, or Galbraith's island, whose foundations reveal the crannog's innovative Iron Age construction methods. Huge tree trunks were driven into the bed of the loch, and rocks were heaped up around a rudimentary wooden frame to support it. Then, as the foundations stabilised above the water's surface, circular dwellings were built on top of the frame, first from timber, and later from stone. Crannogs were secure, attractive environments for family groups living and working on the loch, who repeatedly transformed and repurposed the structures through extended periods of renewal. The Galbraiths of Inchgalbraith eventually built a small medieval castle on their crannog, the ruins of which can still be seen amid the undergrowth that covers the island today. Easy to recognise from their lush tree-covered appearance and rough circular shape, numerous crannogs can be seen from Loch Lomond's eastern shoreline between Balmaha and Milarrochy or from the west side around Luss.

A majority of Loch Lomond's islands are prefixed *inch-* deriving from *innis*, a Gaelic word for island, while other elements of their nomenclature reveal a wide range of associations. Inchmoan, or "peat island", served as a source of fuel to the inhabitants of nearby Luss, while Ceardach indicates

the site of an Iron Age bloomery or furnace. Many islands have early Christian connections: Inchcailloch, the "island of nuns", is so called due to the convent once located here, while Inchmurrin takes its name from a chapel dedicated to Paisley's patron, Saint Mirrin. But piety and criminal activity frequently coexisted around Loch Lomond's shores. The islands were well known for their secrecy and security, making them ideal spots for the illegal distillation of whisky. Samuel Taylor Coleridge visited one such illicit still near Inveruglas in 1803, and happily took a welcome dram. Later in the century, the whisky industry was regulated, and the old illicit still on Inchfad became one of the first government-registered distilleries.

"A FLASH OF IMAGES FROM ANOTHER WORLD"

It is not just humans who enjoy the offerings of Loch Lomond's islands. In 1940, the then Lady Colquhoun had her summer retreat on Inchconnachan and introduced a group of wallabies to the island. Now one of the few viable populations of this small marsupial outside Australia, the descendants of the original wallabies share their home with numbers of capercaillie – Scotland's giant grouse. Despite earlier fears that one of these populations might threaten the presence of the other, wallabies and capercaillie have now happily lived together on the island for many years. If you land a kayak in one of Inchconnachan's sheltered bays, and take time to explore, you are likely to encounter one or more of the island's rare inhabitants.

Lying close to my home, Loch Lomond is my ordinary landscape and has become part of my everyday experience of walking along the West Highland Way. Yet I still never cease to be surprised by the beauty of the loch and its surroundings through all seasons of the year. I often ascend Conic Hill, stand there on the summit boundary between Lowland and Highland, and feel much as Dorothy Wordsworth must have done when she first beheld the stunning prospect of Loch Lomond's islands. She described the view before her as "so singular and beautiful that it was like a flash of images from another world", with Loch Lomond "scattered over with islands, without beginning and without end ... of every possible variety of shape and surface, hilly and level, large and small, bare, rocky, pastoral, or covered with wood. There were bays innumerable, straits or passages like calm rivers, landlocked lakes, and to the main water, stormy promontories. The character of the scene was throughout magical and enchanting." ᕱᕱ

CÒINNEACH

A stranded colourwork cardigan in the mossy hues of Conic hill.

SIZING TABLE

1st	2nd	3rd	4th	5th	6th	7th	8th	9th	10th	
HIP AND BUST WITH OVERLAPPED BANDS										
(ROUNDED TO NEAREST CM/IN)										
84	**90**	94	**99**	104	**109**	114	**119**	125	**129**	cm
33	**35**	37	**39**	41	**43**	45	**47**	49	**51**	in
LENGTH FROM HEM TO UNDERARM										
24	**24**	25.5	**25.5**	26.5	**26.5**	28	**28**	30.5	**30.5**	cm
9½	**9½**	10	**10**	10½	**10½**	11	**11**	12	**12**	in
SLEEVE LENGTH TO UNDERARM										
42	**43**	43	**44.5**	45.5	**45.5**	47	**47**	48.5	**48.5**	cm
16½	**17**	17	**17½**	18	**18**	18½	**18½**	19	**19**	in
UPPER ARM CIRCUMFERENCE										
30.5	**30.5**	32	**32**	33.5	**34**	35.5	**37**	38.5	**39**	cm
12	**12**	12½	**12½**	13¼	**13½**	14	**14½**	15¼	**15½**	in
YOKE DEPTH INCLUDING NECKBAND										
19	**20**	20.5	**20.5**	21	**21.5**	23	**23.5**	24	**25.5**	cm
7½	**7¾**	8	**8**	8¼	**8½**	9	**9¼**	9½	**10**	in
NECK CIRCUMFERENCE WITH OVERLAPPED BANDS										
48	**48**	48	**48**	48	**49.5**	49.5	**49.5**	51	**51**	cm
19	**19**	19	**19**	19	**19½**	19½	**19½**	20	**20**	in

SIZES

Finished bust (with overlapped front bands): 84 (90, 94, 99, 104, 109, 114, 119, 125, 129) cm / 33 (35, 37, 39, 41, 43, 45, 47, 49, 51) in
Shown in the first size with 5cm / 2in positive ease at bust

SCHEMATIC

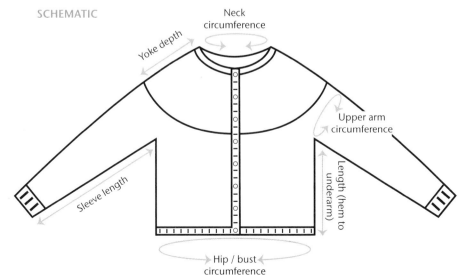

YARN

Kate Davies Designs Milarrochy Tweed (70% Wool; 30% Mohair; 100m / 109yds per 25g ball)
A: Birkin; 9 (10, 10, 11, 11, 12, 12, 13, 14, 14) x 25g balls
All sizes: 1 ball of each of the following 4 shades
B: Bruce
C: Garth
D: Gloamin'
E: Stockiemuir

NEEDLES AND NOTIONS

Gauge-size and below gauge-size circular needles of appropriate lengths for working body, yoke, and neckline.
Gauge-size and below gauge-size needle(s) of your preferred type for working small circumferences.
Stitch markers of two types; 3 'x' and 3 'y', plus 1 for the sleeves.
Waste yarn for holding stitches.
Tapestry needle.
5-9 buttons.
5-9 snap fasteners.
Optional: Bias tape or ribbon for finishing steek edges / front band facing

GAUGE

28 sts and 36 rounds to 10cm / 4in over colourwork pattern **and** stockinette in the round using gauge-size needle. If your colourwork tends to tighten, you may need to change needle sizes to achieve gauge over both stitch patterns.
Gauge was achieved with 3.25mm / US 3 needle.

SPECIAL TECHNIQUES

Steeks – see Special Techniques section on page 126.

PATTERN NOTES

This steeked cardigan is knitted in the round, from the bottom up, all in one piece. The body is knitted first, followed by the sleeves, before joining together and working the colourwork yoke from a chart. After the garment is completed, steeks are cut, and front bands added. Where only one number is given this applies to all sizes.

CHART NOTES

Read each row of the chart from right to left throughout.

ABBREVIATIONS

Standard abbreviations appear on the inside back cover.

INSTRUCTIONS

1

CAST ON, SET UP STEEK AND SIDE MARKERS, WORK CORRUGATED RIB

With below gauge-size needle and shade A, cast on 235 (251, 263, 275, 291, 303, 319, 331, 347, 359) sts and join for working in the round.

Set-up round: K4, pmx, k57 (61, 64, 67, 71, 74, 78, 81, 85, 88), pmy, k112 (120, 126, 132, 140, 146, 154, 160, 168, 174), pmy, k57 (61, 64, 67, 71, 74, 78, 81, 85, 88), pmx, k5.

9 steek sts are now set up between x markers with round commencing at centre of steek (add another marker to indicate beginning of round if required); these sts are worked in stockinette throughout; fronts and back are divided by y markers.

Purl 1 round.

Knit 1 round.

Join in B and work corrugated rib as foll:

Next round: (K1B, k1A) twice, slmx, *k2B, p2A; rep from * to 2 sts before next x marker slipping y markers as you pass them, k2B, slmx, (k1A, k1B) twice, k1A.

Last round sets 2x2 corrugated rib with alternating stripe across steek sts.

Keeping corrugated rib and steek correct as est, rep last round once more.

Break B.

Maintaining A sts as est, work 2 rounds of corrugated rib with C and A, followed by 2 rounds with D and A, then 2 rounds with E and A. *8 rounds of corrugated rib completed.*

Break E and continue with A only.

2

WORK BODY

Change to gauge-size needle. With A, work in stockinette (knitting every round) until garment from cast-on edge measures 24 (24, 25.5, 25.5, 26.5, 26.5, 28, 28, 30.5, 30.5) cm / 9½ (9½, 10, 10, 10½, 10½, 11, 11, 12, 12) in, or your desired length to underarm.

Moving sts around needle without knitting, and removing y markers when you encounter them, sl 4 (4, 5, 5, 6, 6, 7, 7, 8, 8) sts each side of each y marker to waste yarn for underarms. *8 (8, 10, 10, 12, 12, 14, 14, 16, 16) sts on hold at each underarm; 210 (226, 234, 246, 258, 270, 282, 294, 306, 318) sts rem plus 9 steek sts.*

Set body aside.

3 WORK SLEEVES

With below gauge-size needle of your preferred type for working small circumferences and A, cast on 52 (52, 52, 52, 56, 56, 56, 56, 60, 60) sts, pm, and join for working in the round.
Knit 1 round.
Purl 1 round.
Knit 1 round.
Join in B.
Next round: *K2B, p2A; rep from * to end.
Last round sets 2x2 corrugated rib.
Keeping corrugated rib correct as est, rep last round a further 3 times. Break B.
Maintaining A sts as est, work 4 rounds of corrugated rib with C and A, followed by 4 rounds with D and A, then 4 rounds with E and A. *16 rounds of corrugated rib completed.*
Break E, change to gauge-size needle and continue with A only.
Knit 1 round.
Step 1 (increase): K1, m1, k to 1 st before end of round, m1, k1. *2 sts inc.*
Step 2: Knit 6 rounds.
Rep steps 1 and 2 a further 15 (15, 17, 17, 17, 18, 20, 22, 22, 23) times. *32 (32, 36, 36, 36, 38, 42, 46, 46, 48) sts inc; 84 (84, 88, 88, 92, 94, 98, 102, 106, 108) sts total.*
Knit all rounds until sleeve measures 42 (43, 43, 44.5, 45.5, 45.5, 47, 47, 48.5, 48.5) cm / 16½ (17, 17, 17½, 18, 18, 18½, 18½, 19, 19) in from cast-on edge or your desired length to underarm.
Moving sts around needle without knitting, sl 4 (4, 5, 5, 6, 6, 7, 7, 8, 8) sts each side of marker to waste yarn for underarms. *8 (8, 10, 10, 12, 12, 14, 14, 16, 16) sts on hold at each underarm; 76 (76, 78, 78, 80, 82, 84, 88, 90, 92) sts rem.*
Set sleeve aside. Make another sleeve in the same way.

4 JOIN BODY AND SLEEVES INTO YOKE

With longer gauge-size needle and A, join body and sleeves into yoke as foll:
K4 steek sts, slmx, k53 (57, 59, 62, 65, 68, 71, 74, 77, 80) front sts, pmy, k76 (76, 78, 78, 80, 82, 84, 88, 90, 92) sleeve sts, pmy, k104 (112, 116, 122, 128, 134, 140, 146, 152, 158) back sts, pmy k76 (76, 78, 78, 80, 82, 84, 88, 90, 92) sleeve sts, pmy, k53 (57, 59, 62, 65, 68, 71, 74, 77, 80) front sts, slmx, k5 steek sts. *362 (378, 390, 402, 418, 434, 450, 470, 486, 502) sts plus 9 steek sts.*

5 PREPARATORY YOKE SHAPING

Read through the following lettered steps very carefully, then work preparatory yoke shaping for your size. From hereon, the 9 steek sts **are not** included in st count totals.

Step P: *K to 3 sts before y marker, ssk, k1, slmy, k1, k2tog; rep from * a further 3 times, k to end. *8 sts dec.*
Step Q: K to y marker, slmy, k1, k2tog, *k to 3 sts before next y marker, ssk, k1, slmy, k1, k2tog; rep from * once more, k to 3 sts before next y marker, ssk, k1, slmy, k to end. *6 sts dec.*
Step R: K to first y marker, slmy, *k to 3 sts before next y marker, ssk, k1, slmy, k1, k2tog; rep from * once more, k to end, slipping final y marker. *4 sts dec.*
Step S: K to first y marker, slmy, k to next y marker, slmy, k1, k2tog, k to 3 sts before next y marker, ssk, k1, slmy, k to end slipping final y marker. *2 sts dec.*
Step T: Knit 1 round.

First size
Work step S once. *1 round worked; 2 sts dec; 360 sts rem.*

Second size
Work step P once, then step T twice. *3 rounds worked; 8 sts dec; 370 sts rem.*

Third size
Work step Q once, then step T once, then step R once. *3 rounds worked; 10 sts dec; 380 sts rem.*

Fourth size
Work step P once, then step T once, then step R once. *3 rounds worked; 12 sts dec; 390 sts rem.*

Fifth size
Work steps P and T twice, then steps S and T once. *6 rounds worked; 18 sts dec; 400 sts rem.*

Sixth size
Work steps P and T 3 times. *6 rounds worked; 24 sts dec; 410 sts rem.*

Seventh size
Work steps P and T 5 times. *10 rounds worked; 40 sts dec; 410 sts rem.*

Eighth size
Work steps P and T 6 times, then steps S and T once.
14 rounds worked; 50 sts dec; 420 sts rem.

Ninth size
Work steps P and T 7 times. *14 rounds worked; 56 sts dec; 430 sts rem.*

Tenth size
Work steps P and T 9 times. *18 rounds worked; 72 sts dec; 430 sts rem.*

CHART

ALL sizes resume:
K1 (1, 3, 3, 4, 4, 5, 4, 5, 6) rounds, removing y markers as you encounter them.

KEY

- ▢ A: Birkin, k
- ◼ B: Bruce, k
- ▨ C: Garth, k
- ◼ D: Gloamin', k
- ▢ E: Stockiemuir, k
- ⦿ p in shade indicated
- ◪ cdd in shade indicated

6 WORK YOKE CHART

Join in B.
Work 4 steek sts in alternating stripe pattern, slmx, then work 36 (37, 38, 39, 40, 41, 41, 42, 43, 43) reps of chart row 1 to next marker, slmx, work 5 steek sts in alternating stripe pattern. Last round sets chart placement with steek sts. Changing shades and working decreases as indicated, shifting to smaller circular needle as yoke circumference reduces, continue as est and work chart rounds 2-53. *216 (222, 228, 234, 240, 246, 246, 252, 258, 258) sts dec; 144 (148, 152, 156, 160, 164, 164, 168, 172, 172) sts rem.*

7 FINAL YOKE DECREASES

With A, all sizes knit one round.
Following instructions for your size, work final decrease round as foll:

First size
K3, k2tog, (k6, k2tog) 17 times, k3. *18 sts dec; 126 sts rem.*

Second size
[K4, k2tog (k5, k2tog) 3 times] 4 times, [k4, k2tog, (k5, k2tog) twice] twice. *22 sts dec; 126 sts rem.*

Third size
K2tog, (k4, k2tog) 25 times. *26 sts dec; 126 sts rem.*

Fourth size
K5, k2tog, (k3, k2tog) 29 times, k4. *30 sts dec; 126 sts rem.*

Fifth size
[K2, k2tog, (k3, k2tog) 3 times] 4 times, [k2, k2tog, (k3, k2tog) twice] 6 times. *34 sts dec; 126 sts rem.*

Sixth and seventh sizes
[K2, k2tog, (k3, k2tog) 5 times] 4 times, [k2, k2tog, (k3, k2tog) 4 times] twice. *34 sts dec; 130 sts rem.*

Eighth size
[K3, k2tog, (k2, k2tog) twice] 6 times, (k2, k2tog, k3, k2tog) 10 times. *38 sts dec; 130 sts rem.*

Ninth and tenth sizes
[K2, k2tog, (k3, k2tog) twice] twice, (k2, k2tog, k3, k2tog) 16 times. *38 sts dec; 134 sts rem.*

8 WORK NECK EDGING

With below gauge-size needle, join in B, and working steek in alternating stripe pattern throughout (as per hem), k4 steek sts, slmx, *k2B, p2A; rep from * to 2 sts before marker, k2B, slmx, k5 steek sts.
Last round sets 2x2 corrugated rib and steek pattern.
Keeping corrugated rib correct as est, rep last round once more. Break B.
Maintaining A sts as est, work 2 rounds of corrugated rib with C and A, followed by 2 rounds with D and A, then 2 rounds with E and A. *8 rounds of corrugated rib completed.*
Break E and continue with A only.
Knit 1 round.
Purl 1 round.
Knit 1 round.
Bind off all sts in pattern.

9 CUT STEEK; WORK FRONT BANDS

Following instructions in Special Techniques section (or using your preferred method) reinforce and cut steek up the centre stitch.
If you have added / removed length to / from the body you will need to pick up extra / fewer sts accordingly. **The following st counts are for guidance** – work puk at a rate of 3 sts to every 4 rows for front bands, ensuring the final st count is a multiple of 4 + 2.

For the Left Front edge: From the RS, with A, using below gauge-size needle, and picking up sts in the gap between final st of rep and first st of steek, puk 118 (118, 122, 122, 126, 126, 134, 138, 146, 150) sts down left front edge opening. Beginning with a WS row, starting and ending with k2A, and working in same shade sequence as hem and neckline, work 2x2 corrugated rib pattern for 8 rows. Break E and with A only purl 2 rows. Bind off.

For the Right Front edge: From the RS, with A, using below gauge-size needle, and picking up sts in the gap between final st of rep and first st of steek, puk 118 (118, 122, 122, 126, 126, 134, 138, 146, 150) sts up right front edge opening.

Beginning with a WS row, work corrugated rib pattern for 8 rows. Break E and with A only purl 2 rows. Bind off.

10 FINISHING

Graft together 2 sets of sts at underarms. Soak garment in cool water for 20-30 minutes. Rinse and remove excess water. Shape to dimensions given on schematic, paying close attention to ribbing, pin out, then leave to dry (flat or over dress form). Trim back steek edges, cover with tape or ribbon, pin into place, and stitch down using an invisible slip stitch. Stitch 5-9 (quantity depending on your preference) snap fasteners into place on bands. Stitch 5-9 buttons into position, corresponding to fasteners.

Enjoy your Còinneach cardigan!

THE SHIELING

I t's a quiet, crisp afternoon, and I'm walking a stretch of
the West Highland Way out from Rowardennan. This
shore frames what is surely one of the best of Loch Lomond's
many fine views, looking north to the head of the loch,
towards Glen Falloch and the hills beyond. Curving round
the lochside, the path enters an area of lush woodland, then
crosses Ardess Burn. I am walking in the shadow of Ben
Lomond, Scotland's most southerly Munro – and beneath
these oaks, these rowans, it is dark. I turn to take the mountain
path and begin a short, steep ascent. The sunlit prospect looks
inviting, but I'm not going up the Ben today. Instead, I pass
through the wooden gate on the right which stops the deer,
and enter another landscape.

Things are somehow different here: a tilt in the land, a shift
in perspective. The trees thin out, there's a rough levelled
hollow – and is that what remains of a low wall? Turf mounds,
groups of stones, scoured and smoothed by time, rounded out
by moss so green it seems to glow. Another, smaller hollow: a
byre? A fold? Above the sheltered hollows, a wide expanse of
hillside stretches away upwards, and the burn trickles down
conveniently beside the heaped-up stones. Beneath my feet, a
footing. The old location of a shieling.

SEASONAL TRANSHUMANCE

Until the nineteenth century's early decades, tenant farmers
all over Scotland (with the exception of the northern isles)
participated in a form of seasonal transhumance. As the spring
weather warmed, sheep, goats and cattle were driven up
the hills to higher pastures, and people moved with them,
spending the summer months in dwellings and shelters known
as shielings. This pastoral movement had two related purposes:
to divide the grazing animals from food crops cultivated at
lower levels, and to create seasonal dairy produce to support
the permanent settlements below. Life on the mountainside
might be tough, and shieling work was generally the province
of a community's hale and hearty. At the shielings, countless
young men and women of the Highlands and islands happily
spent their summer months – and it's no coincidence that, in

popular tale and song, shielings most often appear as a spaces of pleasure and sexual freedom. In the beautiful Gaelic song *Bothan Àrigh am Bràigh Raithneach* (The Shieling on the Braes of Rannoch), for example, a young woman articulates desire refreshingly frankly: *Is tu fheàrr don tig culaidh / De na chunna mi dh'fhearaibh* (you look better in your clothes / than any man I've ever seen), and anticipates her enjoyment with her lover at the braes of Rannoch shieling, described in the song as *am bothan an t-sùgraidh / Is gur e bu dùnadh dha barrach* (the brushwood-enclosed hut of dalliance).

Following the rough trail over the lower slopes of Ben Lomond, my feet trace out the story written in the landscape. Below the stone ruins high on the hillside is an old head dyke, a heavy, protective stone wall which, for the people who lived and worked here, would once have marked the boundary between summer and winter – between life on the settlement or in the shieling. The dyke protected crops from animals: above it, pasture, and below it, rig-and-furrow cultivation. The rigs, built up from heaped-up compost and manure, made fertile strips for raising crops, while the furrows encouraged drainage as well as separating one plot from another. Maintenance of the rigs was the work of the whole community rather than a single pair of hands, and before each growing season lots were drawn to decide upon the allocation of each strip. Beyond the old runrig, a little further down the hillside, I come across the footings of old autumn and winter dwellings, together with the remains of kilns, bloomeries and platforms once used for drying barley, manufacturing charcoal and working iron and other metals. Such processes demanded intensive use of timber. Long before the current work of conservation in this area began, local woodland would have been carefully managed by the local population for this purpose.

CLEARANCE AND "IMPROVEMENT"

From the small settlement by the lochside to the shielings higher up the mountain, there's plenty of evidence that the lower slopes of Ben Lomond once played host to a thriving rural community. So, what changed? By the middle of the eighteenth century, there was a sizeable military presence around Loch Lomond (part of the British attempt to repress the Jacobite rebellions), and this palpable control of the landscape brought with it associated discourses of modernisation and "improvement". Vernacular buildings, like the rough turf-roofed shieling huts which might be repaired and replaced each summer, were regarded by landowners and government agents alike as signatures of Highland backwardness. A visiting "English gentleman", Edmund Burt, was by no means unusual in describing shielings disgustedly as "fuming dunghills removed and fresh piled up again, and pretty near the same in colour, shape and size". Local landowners began to discourage common grazing, and many decided to actively ban the construction and maintenance of their tenants' "primitive" thatch- and turf-roofed shielings. Families were displaced, tenants were slowly but forcibly removed, and the land around Ben Lomond was put to other uses. Parish records reveal how, in this period, the local population underwent a startling decline. By the early decades of the nineteenth century, fewer than half the people lived by east Loch Lomondside than had done so fifty years before.

CHANGES IN THE LAND

So, what happened to the landscape when communal grazing at the shieling ceased? A ruined shepherd's dwelling on the mountain slopes (larger than the old huts) suggests the presence of sheep on a larger, much more concentrated scale, while more recent forest planting, and the ever-present local deer, point to the increasing use of the lochside during the second half of the nineteenth century for what was then called "sport". The gables and towers of nearby Rowardennan Youth Hostel betray its original purpose as a Victorian hunting lodge. The purposeless ostentation of this building stands in stark contrast to the simplicity of the vernacular architecture it displaced.

If you'd like to get a sense of what Ben Lomond's shielings might once have looked like, volunteers working with the mountain ranger service have constructed a cruck-framed building completely from scratch, which can be seen at the foot of the mountain behind the National Trust for Scotland lodge. Whatever the weather, however harsh the season, the interior of this modest building always suggests complete cosiness. The curved timbers ("crucks" or "couples") take the huge weight of the turfed roof away from the side walls in an efficient act of domestic engineering. Seasonally renewed from the surrounding landscape as the years go by, this small dwelling is, just like the natural world around it, in a continual process of renewal and decay. I have a particular fondness for such buildings of turf and thatch – from the blackhouses of the Hebrides to Icelandic *torfbær* – and this modern reconstruction is a very beautiful example. I often stop here, mentally thank the volunteers for their labour, and think about life in the summer by the shieling. ☉☉

Edward Thomas
The Shieling

It stands alone
Up in a land of stone
All worn like ancient stairs,
A land of rocks and trees
Nourished on wind and stone.

And all within
Long delicate has been;
By arts and kindliness
Coloured, sweetened, and warmed
For many years has been.

Safe resting there
Men hear in the travelling air
But music, pictures see
In the same daily land
Painted by the wild air.

One maker's mind
Made both, and the house is kind
To the land that gave it peace,
And the stone has taken the house
To its cold heart and is kind.

THE SHIELING

This modular blanket (a welcome addition to any shieling hut or summer house) features a thistle motif, familiarly used on the wooden signposts and way markers for the West Highland Way.

YARN
Kate Davies Designs Milarrochy Tweed (70% Wool; 30% Mohair; 100m / 109yds per 25g ball)
A: Hirst; 20 x 25g balls
B: Stockiemuir; 4 x 25g balls
C: Campion; 5 x 25g balls
D: Gloamin'; 5 x 25g balls
E: Garth; 3 x 25g balls
F: Horseback brown; 2 x 25g balls

NEEDLES AND NOTIONS
Gauge-size needle(s) of your preferred type for working small circumferences.
Above gauge-size needle (5 or 6 sizes larger than gauge-size needle) for working 3-needle bind off.
2 gauge-size circular needles, 150cm / 60in length for joining blanket strips.
Stitch marker; Tapestry needle.

LAYOUT DIAGRAM

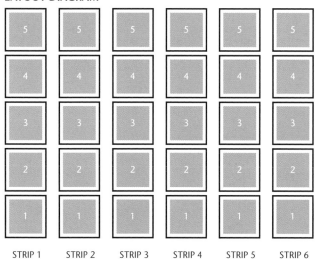

| STRIP 1 | STRIP 2 | STRIP 3 | STRIP 4 | STRIP 5 | STRIP 6 |

GAUGE

28 sts and 36 rounds to 10cm / 4in over stranded colourwork pattern using gauge-size needle(s).

One square to measure: 25.5x25.5cm / 10x10in after blocking. Work a single square for gauge swatch.

Gauge was achieved with 3.25mm / US 3 needle. Above gauge-size needle used for the 3-needle bind off was 5.5mm / US 9.

SIZE

Finished blanket: 140x165cm / 55x65in

SPECIAL TECHNIQUES

Blocking and joining blanket squares; I-cord bind off;
3-needle bind off – see Special Techniques section on page 126

PATTERN NOTES

Each square is knitted in the round from the border inward. The squares are vigorously blocked, joined into strips using a 3-needle bind off and each strip joined to the next to create the blanket. A garter stitch border with mitred edges is then worked in four pieces around the blanket before finishing off with i-cord. When these four small seams are joined the blanket is complete.

CHART NOTES

Read each row of the chart from right to left throughout.

ABBREVIATIONS

Standard abbreviations appear on the inside back cover.

INSTRUCTIONS

1 MAKE SQUARE

With shade A and gauge-size needle(s), cast on 192 sts, pm, and join for working in the round.
Knit 1 round.
Purl 1 round.
Knit 1 round.
Purl 1 round. *4 garter st rounds worked.*
Commence working from chart as foll:
Changing shades and working decreases where indicated, repeating chart 4 times across the round, work chart rounds 1-37. *8 sts rem.*
Break yarn, thread through remaining sts, draw yarn down through the centre of the gathered sts and fasten off to reverse of square.

2 MAKE 29 MORE SQUARES

Following instructions in step 1, make a further 29 squares.

3 BLOCK AND JOIN SQUARES INTO STRIPS

Block squares vigorously, stretching to the dimensions given. Pin each square and leave to dry. If you have blocking wires it is recommended to use them to ensure the sides of each square are straight and firmly stretched.
With RS facing throughout, A and gauge-size needle(s), begin picking up sts along top side of strip 1, square 1 (see layout diagram).
Step X: Puk 1 st in corner (lining up with cdd), pup 48 sts along edge, puk 1 st in corner (lining up with cdd) *50 sts.*
With A and second gauge-size needle, repeat step X to pick up sts as along bottom edge of strip 1, square 2.
Placing squares 1 and 2 parallel to one another with RS outwards and needle tips pointing to the right, use above gauge-size needle to work 3-needle bind off across all 50 sts. Break yarn and fasten off through last st.
Following layout on diagram, join squares 3, 4, and 5 to create first blanket strip.
Repeat process for strips 2-6.

KEY

☐ A: Hirst, k
▨ B: Stockiemuir, k
▨ C: Campion, k
■ D: Gloamin', k
▨ E: Garth, k
■ F: Horseback brown, k
⚠ cdd in shade indicated

CHART

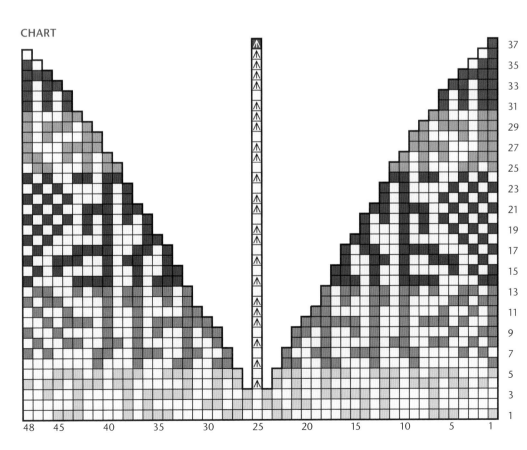

4 JOIN STRIPS INTO BLANKET

When picking up sts along strips, follow step X as est above (i.e., pup along each edge of each square and puk 1 st in each corner join.)

With RS facing, A and longer gauge-size circular needle, puk 250 sts along right hand long edge of strip 1 and then, with second longer gauge-size circular needle, puk 250 sts along left hand long edge of strip 2. Join strips together with 3-needle bind off as est for squares. Continue adding strips to blanket until all 6 strips are joined.

5 WORK LONG EDGES OF BORDER

You will now pick up and work each side of the blanket border separately. When changing shades leave yarn tails at least 10cm / 4in long which can then be used for completing the small mitred seam in step 6.

With RS facing, A and longer gauge-size circular needle, puk 300 sts along first long edge of blanket. One border edge will now be worked back and forth in garter st with increases as foll:

Row 1 (WS): Knit.
Row 2 (RS): Kfb, k to last st, kfb. *2 sts inc.*
Row 3: Knit.
Row 4: Kfb, k to last st, kfb. *2 sts inc.*
Last 4 rows set pattern.
Break off A and join in B.
Work 4 rows of garter stitch and increase pattern as est in following shade sequence: B, C, D, E. *20 sts inc; 320 sts.*
Next row (WS): Join in F and work rows 1-3 of garter stitch and increase pattern. *2 sts inc; 322 sts.*
With RS facing and F, bind off using 2 stitch i-cord method.
Repeat process for opposite long blanket edge.

6 WORK SHORT EDGES OF BORDER

For the shorter blanket edges, referring to step 5, puk 250 sts, and work garter st with increase rows 1-4 a total of 4 times in the same B, C, D, E shade sequence. *20 sts inc; 270 sts.*
Next row (WS): Join in F and work rows 1-3 of pattern. *2 sts inc; 272 sts.*
With RS facing and F, bind off using 2 stitch i-cord method.
Repeat process for opposite short blanket edge.

7 FINISHING

Use yarn tails from border to match shades, carefully join mitred seams together. Weave in any remaining ends to the back of the work. Steam block garter st edging and give joined squares, and whole blanket a final steam on the reverse.

Enjoy your The Shieling blanket!

ROWCHOISH

The West Highland Way wraps itself around the east shore of Loch Lomond. Over stone and twisted tree root, through bog, burn and bracken, the Way covers twenty-six miles along the loch's wonderfully uneven shoreline. The views are always spectacular and the woodland very beautiful. Yet a day's walking can often feel drawn out, and you might well be in need of rest. Tiring between Rowardennan and Inversnaid, you might look out for a narrow muddy path off the main WHW track. Follow the path onwards to a clearing, where in front of you you'll spot a small, old stone building with a new corrugated roof. If you are really lucky, someone will already have lit the fire, and there'll be a smell of woodsmoke in the air. The door to this building is always open, and you'll know you are in the right place because there's a sign painted on it in red letters: *Rowchoish Bothy*.

What is a *bothy*? With etymological roots in the Scottish Gaelic *bothan* as well as the Norn / Shetlandic *böd*, *bothy* is a word that simply means a basic hut or shelter. In Scotland and a few other areas of the UK, bothies are tiny buildings in the remote places enjoyed by walkers, cyclists and all others who enjoy the great outdoors. Sometimes difficult to find, often situated in locations of outstanding natural beauty, after a long day's walking a wee bothy is always a very welcome sight. The doors to these little lonely buildings are always unlocked, and the space and shelter they offer is free for all to use.

How did bothies and the practice of using them – known as *bothying* – first come about? Bothies are generally located at some distance from roads and public transport, in locations that are often hard to find. In Scotland, many of these buildings are found in settlements depopulated during the period of nineteenth-century clearance and emigration, while others began life as the modest homes of shepherds or ghillies whose work brought them to the remote peripheries of Scotland's Highland estates. Abandoned by the early decades of the twentieth century, and in various states of disrepair, bothies began to be used as weekend shelters by the pioneers of Scotland's outdoor movement, whom we first met gathered around the Craigallian Fire on the first stage of our journey. An air of clandestine secrecy

initially surrounded the occupation of bothies by hillwalkers, cyclists and mountaineers, but, as the years went on, the buildings were increasingly used with landowners' tacit or explicit consent. Often, a climbing or walking club (such as the Creagh Dhu) would informally adopt a ruined building, restoring and maintaining it for the convenience of its members.

By the mid-1960s, the idea of a national bothy network was frequently mooted, and the organisational challenge was taken up by Bernard Heath and his friends. In 1965, Heath founded the Mountain Bothy Association (or MBA), with the key aim of maintaining "simple unlocked shelters in remote mountain country for the use of hillwalkers, climbers and other genuine outdoor enthusiasts who love the wild and lonely places". The MBA was financed by a five-shilling annual membership fee and ad-hoc donations, while the work of rebuilding and restoring ruined buildings was voluntary and unpaid. "Members' only reward", an Association memorandum read, "will be the knowledge that their efforts have helped save a bothy from ruin." At the MBA's inaugural meeting, donations were received from outdoor groups all over Britain, and support was enthusiastically offered by national organisations such as the Forestry Commission. The MBA received letters from keen bothiers from as far afield as Iceland, applauding the network as "a smashing idea" and enclosing a donation. With the permission of estate owners, and the understanding of the groups who had previously adopted each shelter, the MBA began to renovate and maintain small buildings all over Scotland, from the Borders to the Cairngorms.

What might one expect from a bothy? Holiday cottages they certainly are not, and probably the best way to think about bothying is as a form of wild camping, with slightly better shelter, and usually added company, in a fairly remote location. There's generally a fireplace, a line on which to hang your sodden socks, plenty of space to dry out (if the weather has proved inclement), and somewhere to sit, cook and sleep. The facilities are basic but, for the weary walker, always welcome: "after 3 nights freezing in my tent in Loch Ossian, it was like being at the Ritz", as one bothy-book entry memorably put it. Scottish mountain bothies have played host to many informal gatherings and even a wedding night, which was notoriously celebrated at Corrour, in 1996. For many years, some bothy locations were veiled in secrecy, as their overuse was feared. But, though you'll still find only a handful of bothies marked on official maps of Scotland, the current era of digital information-sharing seems well attuned to their original spirit, in which the shelters remain open, universally accessible, and free for all to use. In 2015, the year in which the MBA celebrated its fiftieth anniversary, the number of registered bothies listed on its website had grown to over 100, all of which are still maintained by a network of committed volunteers.

The bothy at Rowchoish began life as the byre (animal shelter) of an adjacent cottage. Though the surrounding settlement now lies in ruins, in the mid-eighteenth century Rowchoish was home to nine families. Its name comes from the Gaelic *ruighe* and *coise*, meaning flat ground and foot respectively, suggesting a habitable clearing at the base of the mountain (Ben Lomond). Rowchoish was occupied by at least one household as late as 1930, but by the 1970s was totally deserted. The byre was first renovated by the MBA, with the assistance of the Scottish Rights of Way Society and the permission of the Forestry Commission, back in 1977 and has been maintained by volunteers ever since. Push open the door, and you'll see that the accommodation on offer here is very rudimentary. There's a working fireplace, a large communal sleeping platform, some basic kitchen equipment, and space to cook and rest. You can draw water from the loch or burn (though you should boil it before drinking); and fallen timber in the surrounding woods can be used to feed the fire (though you should never cut down trees for fuel). Just a few yards away, you'll find a pebbled shoreline, from which there's a beautiful view of the rugged landscape through which you'll begin to walk tomorrow. Why not pause here, enjoy the landscape, and drink a dram or two?

Scotland grants everyone the right to open access to the land under what is now one of the most liberal legal frameworks in the world. The Land Reform Acts (2003 and 2016) effectively formalise what has been a long tradition of thoughtful, responsible access to the landscape by all those who love and enjoy the great outdoors. Bothies and bothying play a key role in this continuing tradition. Let's raise a glass to Scotland's mountain bothies and to all those who help maintain them! *Slàinte!* ⊙ ⊙

ROWCHOISH

A cosy wrapigan featuring bobbles, cables and an interesting construction.

YARN

Kate Davies Designs Buachaille (100% Scottish Wool; 110m / 120yds per 50g skein)
Note: Yarn held double throughout
Between Weathers; 9 (11, 12) x 50g skeins

SIZES

To fit bust:
81-97 (102-117, 122-137) cm / 32-38 (40-46, 48-54) in
Garment should be worn with at least 15cm / 6in positive ease
Shown in the first size with 30.5cm / 12in positive ease

SIZING TABLE

1st	**2nd**	3rd	
TO FIT BUST CIRCUMFERENCE			
81-97	**102-117**	122-137	cm
32-38	**40-46**	48-54	in
CABLE PANEL WIDTH			
27.5	**28.5**	29.5	cm
10¾	**10¾**	10¾	in
BACK PANEL DEPTH			
22	**25.5**	26.5	cm
8½	**10**	10½	in
ARMSCYE DEPTH			
20.5	**22**	23	cm
8	**8½**	9	in

SCHEMATIC

NEEDLES AND NOTIONS

Gauge-size and below gauge-size circular needle(s) of appropriate length (minimum 60cm / 24in).
Below gauge-size needle(s) of your preferred type for working small circumferences.
2 spare circular needles, or needle cords, for holding sts.
Cable needle.
Tape measure.
2 locking stitch markers.
Tapestry needle.

GAUGE

14 sts and 20 rows to 10cm / 4in over stockinette worked back and forth with yarn held double using gauge-size needle
16 st cable repeat measures 8.5cm / 3¼in wide
Gauge was achieved with 6.5mm / US 10½ needle

PATTERN NOTES

This slouchy yet structured wrap is formed by fitting a long rectangle comfortably around the body. A long rectangular piece is knitted following a rhythmic cable and bobble pattern, from which stitches are then picked up and knitted downward to form the lower back. When back and fronts are joined together with 2x2 rib, a pair of armscyes are formed, which complete the wrap. Worn open or closed with a statement pin, this is a simple yet effortlessly stylish piece.

CHART NOTES

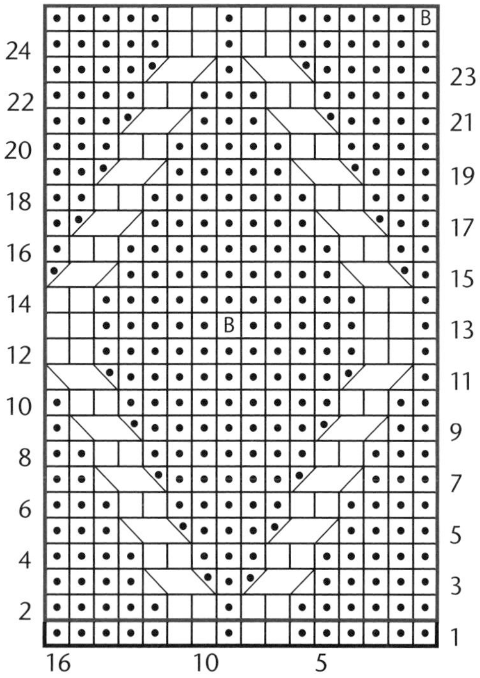

Read right side (odd number) rows from right to left, and wrong side (even number) rows from left to right. Worked flat in rows over 16 sts.

SPECIAL TECHNIQUES

Winding / Turkish cast on – see Special Techniques section on page 126

Make bobble (B)

Row 1 (RS): In next st, knit into front, back, front, back, front to make 5 sts from 1, turn.
Row 2 (WS): P5, turn.
Row 3: K5, turn.
Row 4: P2tog, p1, p2tog, turn.
Row 5: Cdd.

ABBREVIATIONS

B   Make bobble - see Special Techniques listed above.
All other abbreviations appear on the inside back cover.

CHART

(Chart rows numbered 1–24, with columns marked 16, 10, 5)

KEY

☐   knit on RS, purl on WS

▪   purl on RS, knit on WS

B   make bobble

▱   RPC

▱   LPC

☐   pattern repeat

INSTRUCTIONS

1

CREATE WRAP

With gauge-size needle, using the Turkish / winding method, provisionally cast on 52 sts over spare circular needle (or needle cord). Join in working yarn **held double.**
Set-up row (WS): Purl.
Reading from the Chart, work as foll:
Row 1 (RS): K1, work 3 reps of chart row 1, p1, k2.
Row 2 (WS): Sl 2 pwise wyif, k1, work 3 reps of chart row 2, p1.
Last 2 rows set pattern.
Continue in pattern as est, keeping edge sts correct and repeating rows 2-25 of chart until piece measures 107 (117, 127) cm / 42 (46, 50) in from cast-on edge, ending with a WS row. For symmetry, it is nice to end with a row 2 or 24, but not essential.
Break yarn, retaining 52 live sts on spare circular needle or cord. Cast-on sts will later be used for right front, and these live sts for left front.

2

WORK BACK

Using locking stitch markers / safety pins, mark points along left-hand edge as foll:
Measure 33 (35.5, 38) cm / 13 (14, 15) in along edge from cast-on point and pm, then measure 41 (46, 51) cm / 16 (18, 20) in from first marker and place a second marker.
Back is now marked in centre of wrap between markers.
With gauge size needle, puk 64 (80, 88) sts along edge of marked area.
Row 1 (WS): Purl.
Row 2 (RS): K1, m1, k to 1 st before end, m1, k1. *2 sts inc.*
Rep rows 1-2 a further 2 (6, 8) times. *70 (94, 106) sts.*
Continue working back and forth in stockinette as est until piece measures 13 (14, 15) cm / 5 (5½, 6) in from picked-up edge. Break yarn, keeping sts live on needle.

3

WORK RIB WITH I-CORD EDGE

With longer below-gauge size needle, moving sts without knitting them, set up back and fronts for rib as foll: sl 52 sts held from cast-on edge for right front, sl 70 (94, 106) back sts, sl 52 sts held for left front. *174 (198, 210) sts.*

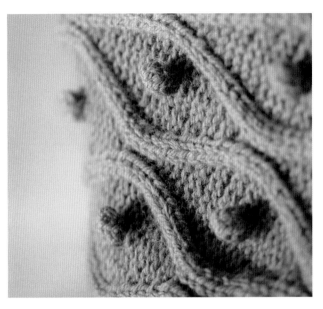

With RS facing, beginning at left front edge, work 2x2 rib as foll:
Row 1 (RS): *K2, p2; rep from * to last 2 sts, k2.
Row 2 (WS): Sl 2 pwise wyif, *k2, p2; rep from * to last 4 sts, k2, sl 2 pwise wyif.
Last 2 rows set pattern.
Keeping 2x2 rib and i-cord edge pattern correct as est, rep rows 1-2 until rib measures 9 (11.5, 11.5) cm / 3½ (4½, 4½) in.
Bind off in rib, binding off the i-cord edges as knit sts.

4

WORK ARMSCYES

With RS facing, below gauge-size needle(s) of your preferred type for working small circumferences, and beginning at underarm point where back meets front, puk 56 (60, 64) sts around armscye.
Row 1: *K2, p2; rep from * to end.
Last row sets pattern.
Rep row 1 a further 6 times.
Bind off in rib.
Work second armscye in the same way.

5

FINISHING

Weave in all ends to the wrong side of the work. Soak wrap in cool water for 20-30 minutes. Rinse and remove water between dry towels. Shape over a dress form or block flat and pin to shape, allowing front edges to overlap slightly in the middle. Allow to dry completely.

Enjoy your Rowchoish!

STRONACHLACHAR

*This darksome burn, horseback brown
Its rollrock highroad roaring down
In coop and in comb the fleece of his foam
Flutes and low to the lake falls home.*

Gerard Manley Hopkins, *Inversnaid*

As you approach Inversnaid, you can hear the waterfall. Through the groves of oaks and birches along the West Highland Way, its muffled roar will reach your ears – and, if you are walking here after a few days of rain, the noise can be astounding. Rushing headlong down the hillside, the sound reminds you that this is a watery landscape whose very substance is defined by its countless burns and rivers, its deep lochs and pools. You might now turn to walk up the hill beside the hotel; stand on the bridged platform high above the cascade and pause to remember the wonderful poem that Gerard Manley Hopkins composed here a century ago. Hopkins' encomium to Inversnaid's "wildness and wet" is startling and heartfelt, but the watery landscape whose praises he sang was, even then, not simply the work of nature but of human ingenuity. If you follow the flow of the water back towards Stronachlachar, you will see how human work and water are uniquely interwoven in the story of this landscape.

To understand this story, we must wind back the clock to 1848, when a cholera epidemic swept through Glasgow, claiming almost 4,000 lives. The city had been struck by the disease before – but, perhaps because this outbreak was particularly indiscriminate, affecting the city's wealthy neighbourhoods alongside the closes and tenements of the poor, there arose a renewed sense of urgency about matters of public health. By mid-century, the work of pioneering contagionists like local doctor James Maxwell Adams was beginning to correct popular understanding of the disease as a bacterial infection spread by contaminated water, not (as was previously thought) by odours or "miasma". At the time of the epidemic, all Glaswegians drank water which had been drawn from the polluted River Clyde through pumps and pipelines which were operated by several different commercial water companies. The city's corporation realised that only radical change would solve the problem of the dirty river water. Through a visionary feat combining innovative engineering with public acquisition, they completely transformed Glasgow's municipal infrastructure, providing a reliable source of clean, fresh water for the city's inhabitants.

By 1852, two enterprising local engineers, William John Rankine and John Thomson, who had conducted careful research into securing "an ample supply of pure water, sufficient not only for [Glasgow's] present inhabitants, but for future generations", were able to present their findings to the city corporation. In the Highland lochs north of Glasgow, they had found water of an exceptionally high potable quality. Just thirty miles away, Loch Katrine offered a convenient natural reservoir whose water was "so clean that filtration might be dispensed with". Rankine and Thomson's proposed method of transporting Loch Katrine's pure Highland water to the city was very simple: gravity. The loch was situated 300 feet above Glasgow (which lies at sea level), and an interconnected system of aqueducts, bridges and pipelines would "substitute the natural descent of water for the costly operation of pumping". To finance the works, Rankine and Thomson proposed the creation of a joint stock company controlled by the city: Glasgow's water supply would be in public hands. The corporation responded to their scheme enthusiastically, appointing John Frederick Bateman to oversee the works and, under the committed leadership of Provost John Stewart, implementing the legal changes necessary to acquire and transform the existing private water companies. The Glasgow Corporation Water Works Act was passed on 12 July 1855. Work on Rankine and Thomson's scheme began, and Bateman rolled up his sleeves to manage the huge undertaking with energy and efficiency.

AQUEDUCTS AND PIPELINES

The first task was to create a small dam to raise Loch Katrine's water level. Then the hard work of constructing pipelines and aqueducts commenced. Tunnelling through the spurs of Ben Lomond required more than sixty drills to be in continuous operation – and, because this was before the operation of pneumatic tools, all work was done by hand. Boring through solid rock, and building high open-cut aqueducts, toiling in their thousands, Bateman's workers steadily created the innovative infrastructure that carried Loch Katrine's water south. The slow descent and regular gradient of the pipeline generated enough pressure to carry around 200 million litres of water every single day over the new bridges crossing the Blane and Endrick valleys. From there, it travelled on to Mugdock, to a reservoir at the city's northern limits. Twenty miles of pipeline were then required to move the water from Milngavie down to Glasgow, and a further forty-six miles enabled it to be dispersed city-wide. With its elegant arched aqueducts, its weirs with obvious echoes of classical architecture, and its decorative, boldly painted ironwork, the Loch Katrine scheme was perhaps the most impressive waterworks the nineteenth century had ever seen. The structure passed through landscapes of extraordinary beauty, and was also in itself an extraordinarily beautiful work of engineering whose elaborate design bespoke awareness of its cultural importance. Certainly, the Loch Katrine aqueducts were a huge source of local pride. Local engineer James Gale, who redeveloped the intra-city pipeline network as part of the scheme, declared: "It is a work which will bear comparison with the most extensive aqueducts in the world, not excluding those of ancient Rome; one of which any city may be proud."

CLEAN WATER FOR ALL

On 14 October 1859, Queen Victoria travelled with great fanfare to Stronachlachar to open the sluices through which the fresh water of Loch Katrine began to flow on down to Glasgow. From a polluted industrial supply that had actively endangered the lives and wellbeing of its population, Glasgow's clean, Highland water was now said to be the best in Britain. According to Hamish Fraser and Irene Maver in their history of the city, "the success of Loch Katrine cannot be overestimated", in terms both of the dramatic improvements in urban health and of the evidence the scheme provided of the benefits of well-managed public ownership. Over the following decades, Glasgow's corporation acquired, renewed and began

to operate the local gas (1869), transport (1872) and electricity (1890) infrastructure, managing the city's resources in the "interests of the welfare of the entire community".

Below where you are standing, just south of the Inversnaid Hotel, you'll see the remains of a concrete structure by the lochside. The heavy materials necessary for the construction of the waterworks were brought up Loch Lomond by barge, landed here and carried up the hillside along an innovative aerial ropeway that was itself powered by water. If you follow the course of Hopkins' "darksome burn" on foot, less than a quarter of a mile up the hillside you'll find an elegant weir, then further on you'll reach the impressive dam at Loch Arklet. From here, you can follow the course of Glasgow's drinking water, underground and overground, to the works at Stronachlachar. Few now pass through these old cast-iron gates to stand and marvel, as many Victorians once did, at the wonders of modern civil engineering. Few now acknowledge the visionary work that's hidden in this beautiful Highland landscape – work that first brought clean, unpolluted water to the people of Glasgow. ۞۞

STRONACHLACHAR

A structured, sinuous and simple tee.

YARN

Kate Davies Designs Buachaille (100% Scottish Wool; 110m / 120yds per 50g skein)
Haar; 6 (6, 7, 8, 9, 10) x 50g skeins

NEEDLES AND NOTIONS

Gauge-size, below gauge-size and above gauge-size needle(s) of appropriate length (60-80cm / 24-32in).
Below gauge-size needle(s) of your preferred type for working small circumferences for sleeve rib.
Stitch markers of two types; 12 'x' and 2 'y'.
Cable needle.
Waste yarn for holding stitches.
Tapestry needle.

GAUGE

22 sts and 32 rows / rounds to 10cm / 4in over pattern using gauge-size needles.
Gauge was achieved with 4mm / US 6 needle.

SIZING

Finished bust: 94 (100, 111, 116, 122, 133) cm / 37 (39, 44, 46, 48, 52) in
To be worn with 5-12.5cm / 2-5in positive ease
Shown in first size with 12.5cm / 5in ease

SIZING TABLE

	1st	2nd	3rd	4th	5th	6th	
BUST CIRCUMFERENCE (ROUNDED TO NEAREST CM/IN)							
	94	**100**	111	**116**	122	**133**	cm
	37	**39**	44	**46**	48	**52**	in
LENGTH FROM HEM TO UNDERARM							
	38	**40.5**	40.5	**43**	43	**43**	cm
	15	**16**	16	**17**	17	**17**	in
ARMSCYE DEPTH							
	20.5	**21**	21.5	**22**	23	**24**	cm
	8	**8¼**	8½	**8¾**	9	**9½**	in
TOTAL LENGTH							
	58.5	**61.5**	62	**65**	66	**67**	cm
	23	**24¼**	24½	**25¾**	26	**26½**	in
NECK CIRCUMFERENCE							
	47	**47**	47	**47**	47	**47**	cm
	18½	**18½**	18½	**18½**	18½	**18½**	in
SHOULDER WIDTH							
	17	**18½**	21	**22.5**	24	**27**	cm
	6¾	**7¼**	8½	**9**	9½	**10½**	in
SLEEVE CIRCUMFERENCE							
	39	**40.5**	42.5	**44.5**	45.5	**47**	cm
	15¼	**16**	16¾	**17½**	17¾	**18½**	in

SPECIAL TECHNIQUES

1x1 twisted rib in the round: *K1tbl, p1; rep from * around.
3-needle bind off – see Special Techniques section, page 126.

PATTERN NOTES

After establishing the six twisted stitch cable panels, this simple tee is worked in the round to the underarms, after which front and back are worked separately, back and forth. The neck is shaped, shoulders are joined with a 3-needle bind off, and ribbing is added around the neck and armscyes.

SCHEMATIC

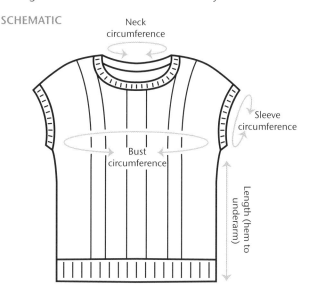

Neck circumference

Sleeve circumference

Bust circumference

Length (hem to underarm)

CHART NOTES

Working in the round: Read all rows as right side rows from right to left.

Working flat in rows: Read right side (odd number) rows from right to left, and wrong side (even number) rows from left to right.

ABBREVIATIONS

Standard abbreviations appear on the inside back cover.

CABLE ABBREVIATIONS

RPT	on RS: slip next stitch to cable needle and hold at back, k1tbl, p1 from cable needle
	on WS: slip next stitch to cable needle and hold at back, k1, p1tbl from cable needle
LPT	on RS: slip next stitch to cable needle and hold at front, p1, k1tbl from cable needle
	on WS: slip next stitch to cable needle and hold at front, p1tbl, k1 from cable needle
RT	on RS: slip next stitch to cable needle and hold at back, k1tbl, k1tbl from cable needle
	on WS: slip next stitch to cable needle and hold at back, p1tbl, p1tbl from cable needle
LT	on RS: slip next stitch to cable needle and hold at front, k1tbl, k1tbl from cable needle
	on WS: slip next stitch to cable needle and hold at front, p1tbl, p1tbl from cable needle

CHART

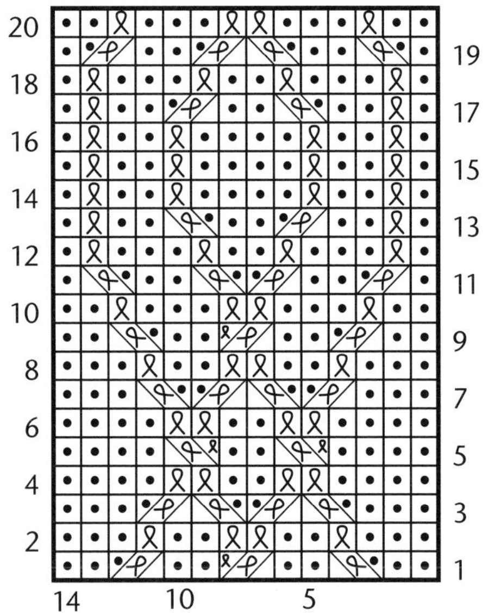

KEY

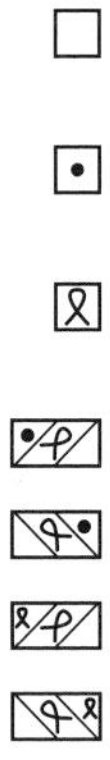

- ☐ knit on RS, purl on WS
- · purl on RS, knit on WS
- Ɐ k1tbl on RS, p1tbl on WS
- RPT
- LPT
- RT
- LT

INSTRUCTIONS

1

CAST ON, PLACE MARKERS, WORK RIB

With below gauge-size circular needle, cast on 204 (216, 240, 252, 264, 288) sts and join for working in the round.

Working in 1x1 twisted rib throughout (see Special Techniques), place markers as foll:

Set-up round: **Work 22 (24, 28, 30, 32, 36) sts, *pmx; work 14 sts, pmx, work 8 (9, 11, 12, 13, 15) sts; rep from * once more, pmx, work 14 sts, pmx, work 22 (24, 28, 30, 32, 36) sts, pmy; rep from ** once more. *2 y markers divide front from back; 6 x markers establish position of cable panels. Last y marker sets start / end of round.*

Work in 1x1 rib for a further 17 rounds.

2

WORK BODY

Change to gauge-size needle, and establish cable panel and stockinette pattern as foll:

Round 1: **K22 (24, 28, 30, 32, 36) sts, *slmx, reading from chart or written instructions, work 14 sts from chart row 1, slmx, k8 (9, 11, 12, 13, 15) sts; rep from * once more, slmx, work 14 sts from chart row 1, slmx, k22 (24, 28, 30, 32, 36) sts, slmy; rep from ** once more. *6 cable panels now established between x markers, divided by panels of stockinette.*

Working the next chart row each round, continue in cable and stockinette pattern as est until piece from cast-on edge measures 38 (40.5, 40.5, 43, 43, 43) cm / 15 (16, 16, 17, 17, 17) in or desired length to underarm, ending with an even-numbered chart row.

3

DIVIDE FRONT FROM BACK

Moving sts around needle without knitting, and removing y markers when you encounter them, sl 102 (108, 120, 126, 132, 144) front sts from LH to RH needle, then sl next 102 (108, 120, 126, 132, 144) back sts to waste yarn.

4

SHAPE FRONT

Working *back and forth in rows*, starting with a RS row, and keeping cable and stockinette panel correct as est, shape front as foll:

Work 2 rows.

Step A (RS): *K to 1 st before marker x, m1r, k1, slmx, work cable panel, slmx, k1, m1l; rep from * twice more, k to end of row. *6 sts inc.*

Step B: Work 7 (9, 9, 9, 9, 11) rows.

Rep steps A and B twice more. *18 sts inc; 120 (126, 138, 144, 150, 162) sts.*
Continue straight in cable and stockinette panel pattern working until front measures 12.5 (13.5, 14, 14.5, 15, 16.5) cm / 5 (5¼, 5½, 5¾, 6, 6½) in from underarm division ending with a WS row.

5

DIVIDE FOR FRONT NECK. SHAPE NECK

Keeping cable and stockinette pattern correct as est, work 40 (43, 49, 52, 55, 61) left front sts, sl next 40 sts to waste yarn, sl next 40 (43, 49, 52, 55, 61) right front sts to spare circular needle.
Working back and forth on left front sts only, work one WS row.
Step A (RS): Work to 3 sts before neck, k2tog, k1. *1 st dec.*
Step B (WS): Work to end of row.
Rep steps A and B twice more. *3 sts dec; 37 (40, 46, 49, 52, 58) sts rem.*
Keeping pattern correct as est, work until left front measures 20.5 (21, 21.5, 22, 23, 24) cm / 8 (8¼, 8½, 8¾, 9, 9½) in from underarm divide.
Leave remaining left front sts on waste yarn.

With RS facing, rejoin yarn to right front sts and work to end of row.
Working back and forth on right front sts only, work one WS row.
Step A (RS): K1, ssk, work to end of row. *1 st dec.*
Step B (WS): Work to end of row.
Rep steps A and B twice more. *3 sts dec; 37 (40, 46, 49, 52, 58) sts rem.*
Keeping pattern correct as est, work until right front measures 20.5 (21, 21.5, 22, 23, 24) cm / 8 (8¼, 8½, 8¾, 9, 9½) in from underarm divide.
Leave remaining right front sts on waste yarn.

6

SHAPE BACK

Pick up back sts from waste yarn, and with RS facing, rejoin working yarn to back.
Return to step 4 and repeat upper body shaping in exactly the same way for back. *18 sts inc; 120 (126, 138, 144, 150, 162) sts.*
Keeping pattern correct as est, continue working until piece measures 20.5 (21, 21.5, 22, 23, 24) cm / 8 (8¼, 8½, 8¾, 9, 9½) in from underarm divide, ending with a WS row.
Moving sts around needle without knitting, sl 37 (40, 46, 49, 52, 58) sts for right shoulder to spare needle, sl 46 sts to waste yarn for back neck, sl 37 (40, 46, 49, 52, 58) sts for left shoulder to spare needle.

7 JOIN SHOULDERS

With above gauge-size needle, and working from the WS, place 2 sets of 37 (40, 46, 49, 52, 58) right shoulder sts parallel to one another and work 3-needle bind off.
Repeat for left shoulder.

8 WORK NECK EDGING

With below gauge-size needle, and beginning at point where right shoulder joins back, sl 46 back sts from waste yarn to needle and k across them, puk 12 sts in left front neck shaping, sl 40 front neck sts from waste yarn to needle and k across them, puk 12 sts in right front neck shaping, pm and join for working in the round. *110 sts.*
Decreasing 8 sts evenly across first round, work in 1x1 twisted rib for 6 rounds. *102 sts.*
Bind off in rib.

9 WORK SLEEVE EDGINGS

With below gauge-size circular needle (of your preferred type for working small circumferences), starting at underarm, puk 84 (88, 92, 96, 98, 102) sts around right armscye, pm and join for working in the round.
Work in 1x1 twisted rib for 6 rounds.
Bind off in rib.
Repeat for left armscye.

10 FINISHING

Weave in all ends to the back of the work.
Soak tee in cool water for 30 minutes. Rinse and remove water between dry towels. Block flat (or over dress form if preferred) adjusting / pinning to dimensions given in sizing table, paying particular attention to cable panels, which should lie flat.
Allow to dry completely.

Enjoy your Stronachlachar!

ROB ROY'S ARMS

A famous man is Robin Hood
The English ballad-singer's joy
And Scotland has a thief as good
An outlaw of as daring mood;
She has her brave ROB ROY!

William Wordsworth, *Rob Roy's Grave*

Strolling along Loch Lomondside, you might have spotted a sign pointing to his cave. You may have seen his image on a poster or brochure, noted multiple references to him in your guidebooks, and perhaps even eaten a dish named after him on the menu of a local pub. Having walked this far along the West Highland Way, it would be difficult to miss the fact that you were passing through "Rob Roy country".

Folk hero, local legend: just who was Rob Roy? **Cattle trader?** Spending summers at the shieling, driving herds over the hills: for Rob Roy, like many Highland men, cattle were his life and livelihood. **Cattle *raider*?** Thief, blackmailer, extortionist: the organiser of an enormously successful bovine protection racket that controlled huge areas of mountain country. **Highland rebel?** Fighting alongside his fellow countrymen in the 1715 Rising, banned even from the use of his own clan name, MacGregor, because of his loyal support of the Jacobite cause. **Harried outcast?** Victimised by men of wealth and influence like the Dukes of Atholl and Montrose; powerful enemies continually sought to undo him but, in the end, were resigned to finding themselves unequal to resourceful, wily Rob. **Ruthless criminal?** Quick to his sword, a vengeful brute not above subjecting his imprisoned captives to near-starvation. **Charming trickster?** Fleet of foot, and adept with both the spoken and the written word, Rob was a gifted escape artist who might slyly slip through any net. **Robin Hood?** Universally admired despite his criminal reputation, Rob was popularly acclaimed for his efforts to support the poor and needy, and for his righting of local wrongs. **Spy and traitor?** As an agent in the pay of the British government, the purported rebel Rob actually sold his secrets to the state in exchange for his own security.

Having already achieved near-legendary status while he lived, by the time he died at Balquhidder (quite peacefully, in his bed), Rob Roy's name was already marked on the new maps which would soon bring Romantic tourists north. Even now, the murky realities of Rob Roy MacGregor are difficult to pin down, and the countless myths surrounding him are perhaps even harder to shake.

ROMANTIC MISREPRESENTATION

In some respects, Rob Roy's legend seems completely generic, and the bold, defiant, hardy Highlander is perhaps simply an example of Eric Hobsbawm's "social bandit": a man of brave ambition, continually persecuted as an outlaw, but celebrated by his community as a rebellious local hero. Yet, seen from a different angle, Rob Roy's story also falls into relief as part of a larger narrative of cultural containment involving the Scottish Highlands and its people. It is no coincidence that popular tales of Rob's derring-do began to draw notoriety at the very moment that his native landscape was brought under occupation and control. General Wade's military roads had begun to cut their way through Rob's familiar cattle-raiding territory, and a garrison filled with British soldiers now stood in near sight of his home by Loch Lomondside.

Like James Fenimore Cooper's last Mohican, Rob is a figure whose "primitive" character can be celebrated precisely because he is on the verge of extinction. And as the rugged Highlander might be exoticised for a Romantic audience, so too might the landscape that he inhabited. At exactly the same time as Rob's contemporaries were being forcibly removed from their homes, so the ruins of Highland depopulation were being papered over with the language of the sublime and picturesque.

But, in a bizarre and long-lasting cultural misunderstanding over his physical size and proportions, might Rob Roy have the last laugh on his own myths, his own Romantic misrepresentation? As early as 1723, the author of *The Highland Rogue, or the Memorable Actions of the Celebrated Robert MacGregor* (which pigeonholed Rob's story within the then-popular genre of criminal biography) was lending his namesake a typically outlandish appearance.

Rob was "a man of prodigious strength of such an uncommon stature that he approaches a gigantic size; he wears a beard above a foot long, and not only his face but his whole body is covered over with red hair". Rob's strength, size and extraordinary hairiness was a theme to which writers of eighteenth-century song and story often warmed – and perhaps no part of Rob was more celebrated than his arms. A few decades later, it seems that English visitors to the Highlands were continually being told about their incredible length; and Dorothy Wordsworth's report that the famous outlaw was said to be able to "garter his tartan stockings below the knee without stooping" is merely one of many similar anecdotes.

By 1817, Rob Roy's physical appearance in Walter Scott's novel echoed that of the cattle he was notorious for stealing: "like a highland bull, hirsute, with red hair, evincing muscular strength", with arms so long he can "without stooping, tie the garters of his Highland hose, which are placed two inches below the knee". Scott bequeathed his long-armed fugitive to future generations – and, ever since, Rob's long arms have proved a favourite feature of numerous biographies, the work of respected outdoor writers, and even public statuary. In 1975, a monument commemorating the Highland rogue was commissioned from Benno Schotz by a MacGregor descendant, to be placed in a prominent position near Stirling Castle.

A JOKE IN GAELIC

Having heard much of Rob's notoriously long arms, Schotz (an otherwise talented local sculptor) endeavoured to accommodate the popular stereotype as best he could. Yet, despite his efforts to create a noble, powerful figure, Schotz made the length of Rob's sword-wielding arm completely outlandish and disproportionate: a gargantuan limb barely seeming to belong to the stocky body beneath it. Could these crazily colossal arms ever *really* belong to Rob Roy? But, any way one looks at it, Rob's long arms never really belonged to him. For they were always mere figurative devices, tropes lost in translation, errors of understanding passed down through the centuries.

The Gaelic phrase *tha gàrdean fada air* – he has long arms – is simply a familiar colloquialism for a thief. Referring to someone as long-armed was an easy way of hinting at someone's questionable trustworthiness; and the familiar embellishment into extraordinary feats of garter-tying has about it a recognisably dry Highland humour. *That's* how long his arms were; *that's* how good a cattle thief he was. Rob's long arms were always rhetorical devices, never literal appendages – and yet, ever since the century in which the Highland rogue lived and died, they have continually dominated his representation in literature, art and popular understanding.

Rob was the fugitive hero we wanted, but we were perhaps foolish to believe all that we were told. We wanted our Highland legends bigger, braver, stronger, even verging on the grotesque, with arms that weren't just long but also *longer than those of any man*. So, when William Wordsworth composed a poem celebrating the exploits of Scotland's brave Rob Roy while standing before what he assumed was his grave, he was actually at Glengyle, far from MacGregor's actual remains in the churchyard at Balquhidder. The Romantic construction and reconstruction of the lost Highlander has been, from the start, a work of continual error and exaggeration. With his outlandishly long arms, charismatic and mercurial Rob Roy MacGregor reaches out of the past to tickle us: a joke in Gaelic, played on the English language, for more than 300 years. ☌☉

HIGHLAND ROGUE

This simple-to knit circular snood features a completely reversible stitch pattern created with knits and purls.

YARN
Kate Davies Designs Buachaille (100% Scottish Wool; 110m / 120yds per 50g skein
Highland Coo; 6 x 50g skeins

NEEDLES AND NOTIONS
2 x gauge-size needles.
Tapestry needle.

GAUGE
20 sts and 24 rows to 10cm / 4in over knit-purl pattern using gauge-size needle.
Gauge was achieved with 5mm / US 8 needle.

SIZE
Finished width: 42cm / 16.5in
Finished circumference: 162cm / 64in

SPECIAL TECHNIQUES
Turkish / winding cast on; Grafting in pattern – see Special Techniques section on page 126.
(3-needle bind off can be used to join ends of snood if preferred)

PATTERN NOTES
The snood is cast on provisionally, and worked in one long piece, with an integrated slipped stitch edging for a neat finish. When the snood has reached the required length, the ends are joined together to create its circular shape.

CHART NOTES
Read right side (odd number) rows from right to left, and wrong side (even number) rows from left to right.

ABBREVIATIONS
Standard abbreviations appear on the inside back cover.

INSTRUCTIONS

1

WORK SNOOD

Using the Turkish / winding method over two gauge-size needles, provisionally cast on 84 sts. Using a single needle, continue as foll:
Set-up row: K2, reading from the chart or written instructions, work 8 reps of chart row 1, p2.
Next row: K2, work 8 reps of chart row 2, sl2 pwise wyif.
Next row: K2, work 8 reps of chart row 3, sl2 pwise wyif.
Last 2 rows set edge and centre pattern.
Continue as est, working subsequent rows from chart or written instructions, always knitting first 2 sts and slipping last 2 sts of each row to create edge.
Work as est until piece measures 162cm / 64in from cast-on edge.

2

FINISHING

Place two gauge-size needles at start and end of snood parallel to one another and, depending on preference, graft in pattern or use 3-needle bind off to join two sets of 84 sts together.
Weave in all ends to the back of the work. Soak snood in cool water for 20 mins, press out water between two towels, pin out to dimensions given and allow to dry completely.

Enjoy your Highland Rogue!

WRITTEN INSTRUCTIONS
Row 1 (RS): P4, k1, p1, k4.
Row 2 (WS): P3, k2, p2, k3.
Row 3: P2, k2, p1, k1, p2, k2.
Row 4: P1, (k2, p2) twice, k1.
Row 5: K2, p3, k3, p2.
Row 6: K1, p4, k4, p1.
Rep rows 1-6 for pattern.

CHART

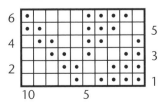

KEY

☐ knit on RS, purl on WS

⊡ purl on RS, knit on WS

ÒRAN DO CHAORA

Hó ró chaora cheannfhionn
Ho ro, the white-faced ewe

eaving Tyndrum, on the West Highland Way, there's
a definite feeling of heading for the hills. Railway, road
and path all run parallel to one another, and – whatever
their mode of transport – everyone seems to be moving
on to higher ground. Across the great wide mouth of Auch
Glen, the landscape opens out, and in front of you there's one
huge conical mountain. In spring, it glows exuberantly green;
in autumn, russet brown; and in winter its steep slopes
are topped with raggedy caps of snow. But whatever the
season, you cannot fail to notice the deep rivulets which
gouge their dramatic course down the peak's western flanks:
the *dobhrag* – or streams – after which the mountain is thought
to take its name.

For this is Beinn Dòbhrain, and the glen where you now
walk was once the home of a poet who famously sang its
praises. The West Highland Way between Tyndrum and
Glen Etive might properly be described as the landscape of
Donnchadh Bàn Mac an t-Saoir, or Duncan Ban MacIntyre, the
great eighteenth-century Gaelic bard, who composed Moladh
Beinn Dòbhrain / In Praise of Ben Dorain.

A GAELIC BARD
Born at Druim Liaghart in 1724, Donnchadh Bàn never learned
to read or write. Employed as a gamekeeper at Glen Lochy
and later at Ais an t-Sìthein by local dukes and earls, he was
a somewhat reluctant Hanoverian. In his early twenties,
Donnchadh Bàn began composing songs and poems, which
he sang and shared with friends and neighbours, carrying their
words around in his mouth and mind. In 1768, after he had
dictated his songs to a Luss clergyman, a print edition of the
poet's works appeared in Gaelic, to considerable local acclaim.
Donnchadh Bàn was known for his mild-mannered, happy-go-
lucky nature, and his songs evince a keen intelligence and dry
sense of humour but are most notable for the powerful and
evocative terms in which he describes his native landscape.

If you are familiar with eighteenth-century and early
nineteenth-century verse in English, then the Gaelic songs of
Donnchadh Bàn might come as something of a surprise, for
his Highland poetry is as far removed from Georgic accounts
of landscape as it is from the Romantic picturesque. His songs

arise out of an experience of place that's refreshingly palpable and proximate — his is a landscape that's irrefutably lived, rather than just observed or aesthetically sublimated. As Alan Riach puts it, it is a "vision that is never turned purely to ether but brings itself back to the human and animal, to floral and geological realities, to the interconnectedness of beauty, grace, mortality and food".

SINGING THE LANDSCAPE INTO BEING

In his songs, Donnchadh Bàn tells the stories of the places that he knows through sedulous accrual of their everyday detail. From different kinds of grass, to varieties of nut or insect, each song uses words to celebrate a landscape of accumulated natural riches. Here's one example (of many) from *Òran Coire Cheathaich / Song to a Misty Corrie.*

Do leaca choibhneil gu dearcach braoileagach
Breac le foighreagan 's cruinn-dearg ceann;
An creamh 'na chaithrichibh 'm bac nan staidhrichean,
Stacan fraoidhneasach nach bu ghann;
Am beàrnan-bride 's a' pheighinn-rioghail
'S an canach min geal, 's am mìslean ann –
'S a h-uile mìr dheth o'n bhun as ìsle
Gu h-ionad cireann na crìch' as aird'.

Your welcoming braes abound with blaeberries and lingonberries,
Speckled with round, red cloudberry mounds
On each step, a clump of wild garlic
Countless precipices, embroidered with flowers
Dandelion and penny royal
Soft white cotton sedge, sweet grasses are there
From the lowest foot of the hill
To the highest rocky headland.

The subject here is the extraordinary biodiversity of a very ordinary Highland landscape, whose berry-concealing braes and magical staircase of wild garlic might appear as mere rock and bog to those who did not know it. The focus of the poet's attention is quotidian, yet elevated into a theme worthy of celebration through the highly ornate diction and very precise use of sound and rhythm that's characteristic of Gaelic song. The poet carefully embroiders the landscape with language, just as the wildflowers adorn the corrie with their colourful blooms.

It's important to understand Donnchadh Bàn's compositions as songs, because sound and rhythm are so essential to their meaning. Many of his works were meant to be sung following the formal pattern of specific Highland musical genres. *Moladh Beinn Dòbhrain / In Praise of Ben Dorain*, for example, is a pibroch, with a theme, variations and embellishments. Spoken aloud, Alan Riach's recent translation gives a good sense of the song's mesmeric rhythmic effects in English:

An t-urram thar gach beinn
Aig Beinn Dòbhrain;
De na chunnaic mi fo 'n ghréin,
'S i bu bhòidhche leam:
Munadh fada réidh,
Cuilidh 'm faighte féidh,
Soilleireachd an t-sléibh
Bha mi sònrachadh;
Doireachan nan geug,
Coill' anns am bi feur.

Praise over all to Ben Dorain –
She rises beneath the radiant beams of the sun –
In all the magnificent range of the mountains around,
So shapely, so sheer are her slopes, there are none
To compare; she is fair, in the light, like the flight
Of the deer, in the hunt, across moors, on the run,
Or under the green leafy branches of trees, in the groves

A pibroch is *ceòl mòr* / great music: a complex, extended art form meant to elevate its subject. Here, *ceòl mòr* displays the poet's facility with Beinn Dòbhrain's majesty and splendour just as much as its environmental detail.

Taken as a whole, Donnchadh Bàn's œuvre might be read as a singing of his beloved landscape into being. Each song retells a place, remakes it, through its own precise ecological litany. Yet this Highland landscape is by no means wild or free, but deeply imbricated with the human, thriving under good stewardship and revolting under mismanagement. Human community and culture were important themes for Donnchadh Bàn too, and his songs celebrated the domestic daily life of the Highlands just as much as its natural world.

Those who make with textiles, just like those who make with words, understand how human creative endeavour can be closely bound up with a sense of place. With wool, the connection between land and process is perhaps particularly acute: grown and clipped from grazing animals, spun into yarn, knitted or woven into cloth, wool can literalise the fabric of landscape. Donnchadh Bàn clearly understood this. His *Òran do Chaora / Song to a Ewe* is a joyous celebration of the ordinary fabric of his community and of the everyday labour of the women who worked with wool.

The ewe celebrated in this tragi-comic song is a pretty white-faced creature that the poet received as a gift from his neighbour, Susie. This wondrous animal was fertile (giving birth to two lambs every year), healthy (her milk providing

delicious cream and crowdie) and spirited (always at the head of the flock as it moved to and from the village). As well as growing fabulously bouncy wool which could be spun into soft yarn, the ewe's fleece also provides the poet with the odd fly, which he happily uses to catch fish. But one day, he discovers the ewe's remains in Allt Ghartain, where she has been killed by a fox. The poet feels the loss keenly:

'N uair a shuidheas mi air tulaich
'S turraman a bhios air m' aire

A' cuimhneachadh coslas na caorach
Nach robh h-aogas anns an fhearann.

Bha i riabhach, 's bha i lachdann,
Bha i caisfhionn, 's bha i ceannfhionn;

...

'S misde mi gun d' rinn i m' fhàgail,
'S b' fheàirrde mi i 'm fad 's a dh' fhan i.

Cha do leig i riamh an fhàilinn
Ann am fhàrdaich fhad 's a mhair i

'N uair a rachainn chun a h-àirigh
Chuireadh i na tràthan tharam.

When I sit upon a hillock,
'tis on grief my mind is focused

recalling the image of the ewe
that had no equal in the country.

She was brindled, she was tawny,
she was white-footed and white-faced;

...

I am the poorer for her passing,
I was the better of her while she lived.

She never, while she lived, permitted
scarcity within my dwelling

Whenever I went to the shieling,
she would tide me over meal times.

How, then, without the white-faced ewe, would the poet find a good fleece from which fine cloth for his coat might be woven? He decides to go "thigging" for raw wool around the households of Glen Etive (rather than begging, "thigging" might be understood as a neighbourly exchange, in which favours were swapped for company, songs and stories). Moving from house to house, the poet relates the sorry tale of the white-faced ewe to the women of Glen Etive, accepts some wool from each, and takes a dram "to shake the sadness off". The fleeces, which each woman gladly offers him in compensation for his loss, are carded, spun and sent off "to the shuttle". As the gathering of the wool is a shared community endeavour, so too its finishing becomes a collective enterprise, as the women of Glen Etive join together to full the woven cloth.

THE SHARED LABOUR OF WOMEN

Òran do Chaora is written as a waulking song: a melody which women of the Scottish Highlands and islands sang together, as they agitated lengths of woollen cloth to full, soften and finish prior to its use for household rents or domestic manufacture. Waulking songs alternated between short verses (sung by an individual, and often spontaneously improvised) and a chorus (in which everyone would join). Accompanied as they were by vigorous physical activity as the women jostled together, loudly thumped the table and moved the cloth around the room, waulking could be a riotous affair, and its songs were often associated with wild exaggeration, rudeness and much hilarity.

So, perhaps rather than the white-faced ewe after whom it is named, Donnchadh Bàn's song is in fact an encomium to the women of his community, and to their shared labour:

Bidh a tùrn an làimh gach té dhiubh
'S bidh a beul a' seinn na h-ealaidh.

Té ri bùrn is té ri mòinidh,
Té a' cur seòl air an ainneal;

Té 'ga phostadh ann an tuba,
Té 'ga luidreadh, té 'ga ghlanadh;

Dithis 'ga shlacadh gu làidir,
Dithis 'ga fhàsgadh gu grammail.

Each of them takes her task in hand,
while her mouth will sing the music.

One sees to water, one to peats,
another keeps the fire well trimmed;

One tramps it in a tub,
one steeps it and one rinses it;

A couple pound it with vigour,
and a couple wring it with strong grasp.

In the inventive manner that's entirely characteristic of his songs, Òran do Chaora very precisely *enacts* the locale and activities that the poet describes. For, as John Murray has carefully observed, the circular journey Donnchadh Bàn takes through the different settlements and homes of Glen Etive very obviously mirrors the passage of the woven cloth from hand to hand: "the poet moves around the landscape like cloth being fulled and passed clockwise ... around a fulling board". Just like the women whose strong hands transform the wool they've gathered into finished cloth, so Òran do Chaora is a songline of the human community of Glen Etive, effectively weaving the place into being and memory. And in that act of collective gathering, making and weaving, so the poet too is woven and remade. "Then indeed I shall be clothed", he happily concludes, "by the wool that I collected" ('S ann an sin a théid mo chòmhdach / Leis a' chlòimh a rinn mi theanal).

At Bridge of Orchy, the West Highland Way leaves Beinn Dòbhrain behind and turns towards Inveroran. If you leave the path here, about a mile west of Loch Tulla, you'll find a small plaque commemorating the man who was born at the croft which once stood here: Donnchadh Bàn, the bard of Glen Orchy and Glen Etive. The verse on the plaque reads:

Bidh sinn beò an dòchas ra-mhath
Gum bi chùis na 's fheàrr an t-ath-là,
Gum bi gaoth is grian is talamh
Mar as math leinn air na sléibhtibh.

We will live in hope unfailing
that matters will be better tomorrow
and that wind, sun and terrain
will favour us, on the mountain. ⊙⊙

ÒRAN DO CHAORA

A cropped cardigan with twisted-stitch cable panels and seamless saddle shoulder shaping.

YARN

Kate Davies Designs Buachaille (100% Scottish Wool; 110m / 120yds per 50g skein)

Yaffle; 7 (8, 9, 9, 10, 12) x 50g skeins

SIZING TABLE

	1st	2nd	3rd	4th	5th	6th	
HIP AND BUST WITH OVERLAPPED BUTTON BANDS (ROUNDED TO NEAREST CM/IN)							
	89	96	104	111	120	130	cm
	35	38	41	44	47	51	in
LENGTH FROM HEM TO UNDERARM							
	25.5	25.5	28	28	30.5	33	cm
	10	10	11	11	12	13	in
WRIST CIRCUMFERENCE							
	22	22	23	24	24	24.5	cm
	8¾	8¾	9	9¼	9¼	9½	in
SLEEVE LENGTH TO UNDERARM							
	43	43	45.5	47	47	48	cm
	17	17	18	18½	18½	19	in
UPPER ARM CIRCUMFERENCE							
	30.5	32	33	34.5	35.5	37	cm
	12	12½	13	13½	14	14½	in
FRONT YOKE DEPTH INCLUDING NECKBAND							
	21	21	22	23.5	25	27.5	cm
	8¼	8¼	8¾	9¼	9¾	10¾	in
BACK YOKE DEPTH INCLUDING NECKBAND							
	22.5	22.5	24.5	26	28	30	cm
	9	9	9½	10¼	11	12	in
NECK CIRCUMFERENCE WITH OVERLAPPED BANDS							
	46	46	46	46	48.5	48.5	cm
	18	18	18	18	19	19	in

SIZES

Finished measurement at bust / hip: 89 (96, 104, 111, 120, 130) cm / 35 (38, 41, 44, 47, 51) in
Cardigan should be worn with at least 5cm / 2in positive ease

Shown in the first size with 10cm / 4in positive ease at bust.

NEEDLES AND NOTIONS

Gauge-size and below gauge-size circular needles of appropriate lengths for working body, yoke, and neckline.
Gauge-size and below gauge-size needle(s) of your preferred type for working small circumferences for sleeves.
4 locking stitch markers.
Waste yarn for holding stitches.
Tapestry needle.
5 buttons.

SCHEMATIC

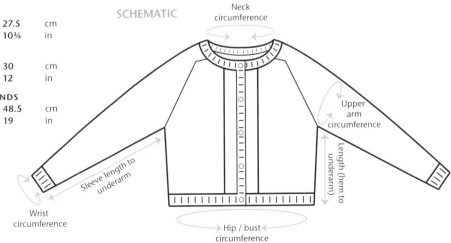

GAUGE

24 sts and 32 rows to 10cm / 4in over stockinette worked both back and forth in rows, and in the round using gauge-size needle. Gauge was achieved with 3.75mm / US 5 needle.

SPECIAL TECHNIQUES

WScdd (wrong side centred double decrease)
1. Slip 1 st as if to knit, slip the next st as if to knit.
2. Placing LH needle through back legs of both slipped sts together, return both slipped sts to LH needle.
3. Insert RH needle through back loops of first 2 sts on LH needle as if to p2togtbl, and slip them together to RH needle.
4. Purl the next st on LH needle.
5. Pass the 2 slipped sts over the purl st and off RH needle. *2 sts dec.*

PATTERN NOTES

This cardigan is knitted seamlessly from the bottom up. Fronts and back are worked together in one piece to the underarms, then divided to work separately. Two sleeves are knitted in the round, then, after joining to the body, the yoke is worked in one piece and shaped using a combination of raglan and saddle shaping. After the neckline is bound off, buttonhole and button bands are added.

Where only one number is given this applies to all sizes.

CHART NOTES

Working flat in rows: Read right side (odd number) rows from right to left, and wrong side (even number) rows from left to right.
Working in the round: Read each row of the chart from right to left throughout.

ABBREVIATIONS

Standard abbreviations appear on the inside back cover.

CABLE ABBREVIATIONS

RPT   on RS, slip next stitch to cable needle and hold at back, k1tbl, p1 from cable needle; on WS, slip next stitch to cable needle and hold at back, k1, p1tbl from cable needle

LPT   on RS, slip next stitch to cable needle and hold at front, p1, k1tbl from cable needle; on WS, slip next stitch to cable needle and hold at front, p1tbl, k1 from cable needle

RT   on RS, slip next stitch to cable needle and hold at back, k1tbl, k1tbl from cable needle; on WS, slip next stitch to cable needle and hold at back, p1tbl, p1tbl from cable needle

LT   on RS, slip next stitch to cable needle and hold at front, k1tbl, k1tbl from cable needle; on WS, slip next stitch to cable needle and hold at front, p1tbl, p1tbl from cable needle

CHART B

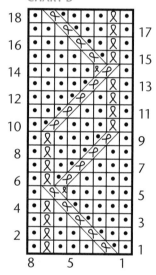

CHART A

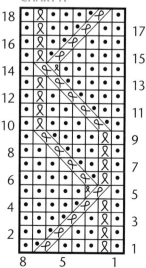

KEY

☐	knit on RS, purl on WS
⊡	purl on RS, knit on WS
⊠	k1tbl on RS, p1tbl on WS
▱	RPT
▱	LPT
▱	RT
▱	LT

INSTRUCTIONS

1

CAST ON, SET UP CHARTS, WORK RIB

With below gauge-size needle, cast on 203 (219, 239, 255, 275, 299) sts.
Row 1 (RS): P1, pm, p1, k1tbl, p4, k1tbl, p1, pm, *k1tbl, p1; rep from * to 9 sts before end of row ending with a k1tbl, pm, p1, k1tbl, p4, k1tbl, p1, pm, p1.
Row 2 (WS): K1, slm, k1, p1tbl, k4, p1tbl, k1, slm, *p1tbl, k1; rep from * to 9 sts before end of row ending with p1tbl, slm, k1, p1tbl, k4, p1tbl, k1, slm, k1.
Last 2 rows set twisted rib and position of cable panels between markers.
Rep rows 1-2 a further 5 times. *12 rib rows total.*

2

WORK BODY, SET UNDERARM STS ASIDE

Change to gauge-size needle.
Row 1 (RS): P1, slm, work 8 sts from row 1 of chart A, slm, k2tog, k to 9 sts before end of row, slm, work 8 sts from row 1 of chart B, slm, p1. *202 (218, 238, 254, 274, 298) sts.*
Row 2 (WS): K1, slm, work 8 sts from row 2 of chart B, slm, p to 9 sts before end of row, slm, work 8 sts from row 2 of chart A, slm, p1.
Last 2 rows set stockinette and cable panel pattern.
Continue straight as est until body from cast-on edge measures 25.5 (25.5, 28, 28, 30.5, 33) cm / 10 (10, 11, 11, 12, 13) in, or desired length to underarm.
Moving sts around needle without knitting, sl 47 (51, 55, 58, 63, 68) sts of right front, sl 8 (8, 10, 12, 12, 14) sts to waste yarn for underarm, sl 92 (100, 108, 114, 124, 134) sts of back, sl 8 (8, 10, 12, 12, 14) sts to waste yarn for underarm, sl 47 (51, 55, 58, 63, 68) sts of left front. *8 (8, 10, 12, 12, 14) sts on hold for each underarm; 47 (51, 55, 58, 63, 68) sts rem for each front and 92 (100, 108, 114, 124, 134) sts rem for back.*
Set body aside.

3

CAST ON SLEEVES

With below gauge-size needle of your preferred type for working small circumferences, cast on 51 (51, 53, 55, 55, 57) sts, pm, and join for working in the round.
Round 1: (K1tbl, p1) 10 (10, 11, 11, 11, 12) times, k1tbl, pm, p1, k1tbl, p4, k1tbl, p1, pm, *k1tbl, p1; rep from * to end of round.
Last round sets rib and cable panel position.

Rep round 1 a further 16 times (slipping markers throughout).

4

WORK SLEEVES

Change to gauge-size needle.
Next round: Sl start of round marker, m1, k to next marker, slm, work 8 sts from row 1 of chart A (for right sleeve) or 8 sts from row 1 of chart B (for left sleeve), slm, k to end. *52 (52, 54, 56, 56, 58) sts.*
Last round sets stockinette and cable panel pattern.

Step A: Slm, k1, m1, k to marker, slm, work 8 sts from next row of chart, slm, k to 1 st before end of round, m1, k1. *2 sts inc.*
Step B: Work 6 rounds, keeping stockinette and cable panel correct as est.
Rep steps A and B a further 9 (11, 11, 12, 13, 14) times. *72 (76, 78, 82, 84, 88) sts.*

Continue as est (without further incs) until sleeve measures 43 (43, 45.5, 47, 47, 48) cm / 17 (17, 18, 18½, 18½, 19) in, or desired length to underarm. Make a note of last chart round worked.

Moving sts around needle without knitting, sl 4 (4, 5, 6, 6, 7) sts each side of start of round marker to waste yarn for underarms. *8 (8, 10, 12, 12, 14) sts on hold; 64 (68, 68, 70, 72, 74) sts rem.*
Set sleeve aside. Make another sleeve, remembering to begin working from chart A (for right) and chart B (for left) sleeve as appropriate, and to end on the same chart round as first sleeve.

5

PREPARE TO SHAPE YOKE

Moving sts around needle without knitting, slip all sts onto single needle, ready to work yoke, marking the 4 sts indicated with locking stitch markers as foll: sl 47 (51, 55, 58, 63, 68) sts of right front, marking final st (M1), sl 64 (68, 68, 70, 72, 74) sts of right sleeve, marking final st (M2), sl 92 (100, 108, 114, 124, 134) sts of back, marking final st (M3), sl 64 (68, 68, 70, 72, 74) sts of left sleeve, marking final st (M4), sl 47 (51, 55, 58, 63, 68) sts of left front. *314 (338, 354, 370, 394, 418) sts.*
Throughout the yoke instructions, these 4 marked sts will be used to position and orientate the shaping.

The yoke is shaped using a combination of decreases, worked over a series of lettered steps described below. Read each lettered step **very carefully**, then follow the instructions for your size, always keeping front and sleeve cable panels correct as est.

Front and back shaping

A (RS): K to 1 st before M1, k2tog (dec from front), k across sleeve, k M2, ssk (dec from back), k to 1 st before M3, k2tog (dec from back), k across sleeve, k M4, ssk (dec from front), k across front to end. *4 sts dec.*

B (WS): P to 1 st before M4, p2tog (dec from front), p across sleeve, p M3, lld (dec from back), p to 1 st before M2, lld (dec from back), p across right sleeve, p M1, p2tog (dec from front), p across front to end. *4 sts dec.*

Raglan shaping

C (RS): *K to 1 st before M1, cdd; rep from * a further 3 times (for M2, 3 and 4), k to end. *8 sts dec.*

D (WS): Purl.

E (WS): *P to 1 st before M4, cdd; rep from * a further 3 times (for M3, 2 and 1), p to end. *8 sts dec.*

Front neck and raglan shaping

F (RS): K2tog, *k to 1 st before M1, cdd; rep from * a further 3 times (for M2, 3 and 4), k to last 2 sts, ssk. *10 sts dec.*

G (WS): Lld, p to last 2 sts, p2tog. *2 sts dec.*

Saddle shaping (short rows)

H (RS, right sleeve): Sl1, work to M2, ssk (1 st dec from back), turn work. *1 st dec.*

I (WS, right sleeve): Sl1, work to M1, p2tog (1 st dec from front), turn work. *1 st dec.*

J (RS, left sleeve): Sl1, work to M4, ssk (1 st dec from front), turn work. *1 st dec.*

K (WS, left sleeve): Sl1, work to M3, p2tog (1 st dec from back), turn work. *1 st dec.*

Closing the gaps

L (WS): Work across row to 1 st before M4, lld, work to M3, p2tog, work to 1 st before M2, lld, work to M1, p2tog, p to end. *4 sts dec.*

6

FRONT AND BACK SHAPING

First size only: Move to step 7.
All other sizes: Work front and back shaping as foll:
Joining sleeves to body on first row, work steps A and B - (1, 2, 2, 3, 5) times. - *(8, 16, 16, 24, 40) sts dec; - (330, 338, 354, 370, 378) sts rem.*

7

RAGLAN SHAPING; FRONT SHAPING

All sizes: Work steps C and E 2 (5, 6, 6, 7, 6) times joining sleeves to body on first row for first size only. *32 (80, 96, 96, 112, 96) sts dec; 282 (250, 242, 258, 258, 282) sts rem.*

Next row (RS): Work steps C and D 19 (15, 13, 13, 12, 15) times. *152 (120, 104, 104, 96, 120) sts dec; 130 (130, 138, 154, 162, 162) sts rem.*
Break yarn. Slip first 9 and last 9 sts of row to waste yarn (setting cable panel sts aside). *18 sts on hold; 112 (112, 120, 136, 144, 144) sts rem.*
Rejoin yarn to right front sts.
Keeping sleeve cable panels correct as est, work steps F and G 1 (1, 1, 2, 2, 2) times. *12 (12, 12, 24, 24, 24) sts dec; 100 (100, 108, 112, 120, 120) sts rem.*

8

SADDLE SHAPING

Work right saddle shaping as foll:
K across right front to M1. Work steps H and I 5 (5, 7, 8, 9, 9) times, decreasing sts from right front and back. *10 (10, 14, 16, 18, 18) sts dec; 90 (90, 94, 96, 102, 102) sts rem.*
Next row (RS): Commence left saddle shaping. Sl M1, work across right sleeve, sl M2, work across to M3.
Now work steps J and K 5 (5, 7, 8, 9, 9) times, decreasing sts from back and left front. *10 (10, 14, 16, 18, 18) sts dec; 80 (80, 80, 80, 84, 84) sts rem.*
Next row: Sl M3, work across left sleeve, sl M4, work across left front to end of row.
Next row (WS - closing the gaps): Work step L ending at right front. *4 sts dec; 76 (76, 76, 76, 80, 80) sts rem.*
Break yarn.

9 PICK UP STS FOR NECK

Change to below gauge-size needle for working neck.

Next row (RS): Rejoining yarn from RS, sl 9 right front panel sts from waste yarn to needle and k across them, puk 4 (4, 4, 4, 5, 5) sts in right front neck shaping, k5 (5, 5, 4, 5, 5) sts across right front, k M1, k15 right sleeve sts, k M2, k31 (31, 31, 31, 33, 35, 35) back sts, k M3, k15 left sleeve sts, k M4, k6 (6, 6, 5, 6, 6) sts across left front, puk 3 (3, 3, 3, 4, 4) sts in left front neck shaping, sl 9 left front panel sts from waste yarn to spare needle and k across them. *101 (101, 101, 101, 107, 107) sts rem.*

10 NECK RIB AND SHORT ROWS

Next row (WS): *P1tbl, k1; rep from * to last st, p1tbl.

Last row sets 1x1 twisted rib.

You will now work short rows to raise the back of the neck in 1x1 twisted rib pattern.

Next row (RS): *K1tbl, p1; rep from * across right front, sleeve and back to M3.

Using your preferred short row method to mark this st, turn, and, keeping 1x1 twisted rib correct as est, work across back to M2, turn; work across back to 1 st past M3 (closing short row gap); turn, work across back to 1 st past M2 (closing short row gap), turn. *4 short rows worked.*
Working each short row 1 st longer than the last as est, work a further 2 (2, 4, 4, 6, 6) short rows. Continue working to end of row (RS) in twisted rib pattern, closing any short row gaps.

Next row (WS): Work a full row in twisted rib pattern, closing remaining short row gaps.
Work a further 6 rows in twisted rib pattern.
Bind off in rib.

11 BUTTONHOLE BAND

With RS facing and below gauge-size circular needle, beginning at hem of right front, puk 3 sts for every 4 rows along right front, being sure to pick up an odd number of sts in total. Make a note of the number of sts picked up. With pins (labelled P), mark out the position of 5 evenly spaced buttonholes along right front edge.

Row 1 (WS): *P1tbl, k1; rep from * to last st, p1tbl placing stitch markers (labelled P) to replace pins.
Row 2 (RS): *K1tbl, p1; rep from * to last st, k1tbl.
Row 3: *P1tbl, k1; rep from * to last st, p1tbl.
Row 4: *Work in rib as est to 2 sts before P, rib 2tog, (yo) 3 times, rib 2tog; rep from * a further 4 times, rib to end. *5 buttonholes made.*
Row 5: *Rib to buttonhole, (rib 1tbl, drop yo, rib 1tbl) into triple yo; rep from * a further 4 times, rib to end.
Work in rib for a further 5 rows.
Bind off in rib.

12 BUTTON BAND

With RS facing and below gauge-size needle, beginning at neck of left front, puk 3 sts for every 4 rows along right front, being sure to pick up the same odd number of sts in total as buttonhole band.
Row 1 (WS): *P1tbl, k1; rep from * to last st, p1tbl.
Row 2 (RS): *K1tbl, p1; rep from * to last st, k1tbl.
Rep rows 1-2 a further 4 times.
Bind off in rib.

13 FINISHING

Weave in all ends to the back of the work. Graft two sets of sts at underarms. Soak cardigan in cool water for 30 minutes. Rinse and remove water between dry towels. Bock flat (or over dress form if preferred) adjusting / pinning to dimensions given in sizing table, paying particular attention to cable panels, which should lie flat. Stitch 5 buttons in place corresponding to buttonholes. Allow to dry completely.

Enjoy your Òran do Chaora!

SEEING RANNOCH MOOR

Rannoch Moor, Rannoch dear.
Beloved best, the best: back here.
      Jackie Kay, *Rannoch Loop* (2017)

There are few landscapes in Britain that arouse negative reactions quite so strongly as Rannoch Moor. Fleeing across its vast expanse in Robert Louis Stevenson's *Kidnapped*, fugitive David Balfour typified the reactions of his Victorian contemporaries to the place:

"much of it was under heather, much of the rest broken up with hags and bogs and peaty pools; some had been burnt black in a heath fire, and in another place there was quite a forest of dead firs, standing like skeletons. A wearier looking desert man never saw."

The language of death and desolation has been a ubiquitous feature of accounts of Rannoch Moor for over 300 years. And, in contemporary travel and nature writing, the moor still appears as a space both malevolent and dreary: "a bald, empty badland", "a wild, dreich desolate place", "150 miles of uninhabited and uninhabitable peat bogs, lochs, heather hillocks, strewn lumps of granite and a few gnarled Caledonian pines", concludes a recently published *Rough Guide,* using much the same language as Stevenson's narrator.

What exactly is it about this boggy plateau, 300 metres above sea level, approximately 82% water, and around the size of Glasgow, that repels its human observers so? Is it because the space of the moor is simply so wide and so expansive? Certainly one thing that seems to bother those looking at Rannoch Moor is that there is not much to see. Accounts of the moor frequently describe an eye searching around for objects of interest which it inevitably fails to find. "Rain all the way", S. T. Coleridge remarked gloomily of his trek across Rannoch Moor to Kingshouse; "add to [this] large moorland pools with bushy islets and *one goat* and you have the whole I saw." Cast free in the moor's unbounded space, Coleridge's eye does not know what

to do with itself and is troubled by the horizon's very ambit. In *The Wild Places* (2007), Robert MacFarlane vividly compares his experience of crossing the wet moor to the "vastness and self-similarity" of a dry desert or an icy tundra: "So extensive was the space within which we were moving that when I glanced up at the mountains ... to gauge the distance we had come it seemed as though we had not advanced at all".

For some, Rannoch Moor's extent suggests not openness, but its opposite – suffocation:

> Here the crow starves, here the patient stag
> Breeds for the rifle.
> Between the soft moor
> And the soft sky, scarcely room
> To leap or soar. Substance crumbles, in the thin air
> Moon cold or moon hot.

In T. S. Eliot's *Rannoch, by Glencoe*, the vast moor stifles, oppresses, allows no room to breathe. Not in any sense a nature poet, Eliot once notably described landscape as "a passive creature", yet his moor is possessed of an obviously maleficent agency, sucking the breath from life itself.

As Eliot compared Rannoch Moor's landscape to the airless atmosphere of the moon, so Walter Scott's friend, the travel writer John McCulloch, likened it to that of a world before time:

"Hideous and interminable ... a desert of vacuity and solitude and death ... an ocean of blackness ... a world before chaos; not so good as chaos, since its elements are only rocks and bogs with a few pools of water."

Unearthly, incomprehensible: while Scotland's mighty mountains might inspire writers with an idea of the sublime, for Eliot and McCulloch, Rannoch Moor simply seems to resist all human meaning. Countless observers of the moor similarly describe a landscape that fills them only with a deepening sense of dread or alienation. So, when the cast of Danny Boyle's *Trainspotting* alight at lonely Corrour station, Rannoch Moor is there simply to reaffirm the group's bald self-estrangement. Whether experiencing the moor in person as a walker, or viewing it from the weatherproof bubble of a train or car, its vast indifference seems to continually trouble our ideas of landscape and humanity.

DESERTS AND PASTURES

Perhaps the very substance of a bog seems hostile: uncongenial to the foot, repelling easy movement. Among these reeds, these rocks, the body is exposed and vulnerable. There's no place for concealment in these dank hummocks, these black lochans. Yet, under the peat, ancient corpses might be found: bogs are places where the human body comes only to die. Faced with a landscape that seems dead, dying or depopulated, the imagination then peoples it with threat. "The phantoms which haunt a desert", wrote Samuel Johnson, "are want, misery and danger, the evils of dereliction rush upon the thoughts, man is made unwillingly acquainted with his own weakness." Johnson, the urbane Londoner, certainly found Scotland's landscape deeply disagreeable, full of such evils:

"An eye accustomed to flowery pastures and waving harvests is astonished and repelled by this wide extent of hopeless sterility. The appearance is that of matter incapable of form or usefulness."

LANSCAPE AND ALTERITY

Johnson's particular problem with the Scottish landscape was that so much of it seemed to him to be unproductive and therefore, from his metropolitan perspective, pointless. Overlooking the fact that locals had long used Rannoch Moor's peat for fuel, its assumed uselessness underlies numerous accounts of the landscape as aesthetically repellent. So, when tourists like Johnson spout invective on the moor's death and black sterility, what they are often really talking about is the apparent resistance of the landscape to "improvement". T. C. Smout has brilliantly explored how intensely negative reactions to Rannoch Moor's "sterile" landscape are bound up with the idea that "peat bog was a desert that needed reclamation or at least was a wasted resource that could legitimately be used for some economically productive purpose". We humans clearly find it hard to understand a landscape that doesn't immediately please us or present itself for service.

Improvers like Johnson's contemporary, Henry Kames, strove relentlessly to drain and fertilise Scotland's moors so that they might better fit such ideas of human purpose. But the bogs retained their dark, watery secrets, and largely remained defiant. Finally, in the past couple of decades, Scotland's bogs and moors have been recognised for their environmental significance and "special scientific interest": inhospitable, nutrient-poor, mostly composed of water, yet surprisingly species-rich. Today, if Rannoch Moor has a purpose, it is to act as nature's last bastion on a crowded island. The literature of travel and tourism now repeatedly describes the moor as "Britain's last remaining wilderness".

I am not alone in loving the boggy, watery world of Rannoch Moor. It is a special place for Robert Macfarlane, for Scotland's Makar, Jackie Kay, and for the highly enthusiastic anonymous author of *Mountain Moor and Loch* (written in 1894 to encourage tourism by train across the newly constructed West Highland Line). I love wide open landscapes – and, to me, Rannoch Moor is twenty square miles of breathtaking beauty in which one can experience a rare feeling of unparalleled lightness and space.

I first crossed the moor on foot walking the West Highland Way in 2005. It was a long day of variable weather, much of it spent in silence, and most of it astounded. Sometimes, when sitting at my desk with an ache in my neck, my body travels outside itself to recall the crick I got that day on the moor,

tramping slowly forwards, gazing out at the endless horizon. Yet the world beneath my feet was perhaps just as arresting as the prospect. Sundew and asphodel, myrtle and juniper. Pops of colour under the dun grasses, bursts of wild fragrance between my fingers. Darting brightly across my path, a beetle with its shimmering petrol-hued armour, a silver slowworm, a lizard the bold colour of an autumn leaf. As Victorian naturalists like Horace Donisthorpe discovered, the brilliant detail of Rannoch Moor's flora and fauna is at least as diverting as its vast size. On a warm summer's day, it can seem lit from within, and during an October sunset, its pools and reeds echo back a whole wide fiery sky. How could Eliot read this landscape as a suffocating absence? Is there anything to fill the heart *more* than the reflections across Loch Bà or Lochan na h-Achlaise on a bright, still winter's day? Samuel Johnson understood an uncultivated moor's alterity as indifference, but why should we expect *any* place to express an accommodating regard for the human? Indeed, perhaps all that this landscape can be said to give us is the opportunity to forget, just for a moment, the stifling smallness of our own humanity. I love Rannoch Moor because it has nothing at all to do with me. Because it is not me. Because it is never the same, but it is always, always itself. ☍

MYRTLE

A delicate lace sweater, named for the beautiful, fragrant highland shrub that grows on Rannoch Moor.

YARN
Fyberspates Cumulus (74% baby suri alpaca; 26% silk; 150m / 164yds per 25g ball)

A: Moonlight; 3 (3, 3, 3, 4, 4) x 25g balls
B: Silver; 2 (2, 2, 3, 3, 3) x 25g balls
C: Water; 2 (2, 2, 3, 3, 3) x 25g balls
D: Slate; 2 (2, 2, 3, 3, 3) x 25g balls

NEEDLES AND NOTIONS
Gauge-size and below gauge-size circular needles of appropriate lengths for working body and neckline.
Gauge-size and below gauge-size needle(s) of your preferred type for working small circumferences for sleeves.
Stitch markers.
Waste yarn for holding stitches.
Tapestry needle.

GAUGE
32 sts and 40 rounds to 10cm / 4in over horseshoe lace pattern using gauge-size needle.
Gauge was achieved with 2.75mm / US 2 needle.
Note: Lace pattern is very stretchy: be sure to wash and block your swatch carefully to ensure you achieve and maintain the correct gauge.

SIZING
Finished bust circumference: 89 (95, 102, 108, 121, 133 cm / 35 (37½, 40, 43, 48, 53) in
For other measurements, see sizing table
Wear with 5-10cm / 2-4in positive ease for a light, comfortable fit. (The garment should skim the body rather than cling to it)
Shown in the first size with 7.5cm / 3in positive ease at bust.

SIZING TABLE

	1st	2nd	3rd	4th	5th	6th	
HIP AND BUST (NOTE: ROUNDED TO NEAREST CM/IN)							
	89	95	102	108	121	133	cm
	35	37½	40	42½	48	53	in
LENGTH FROM HEM TO UNDERARM							
	26.5	29	30.5	33	34.5	34.5	cm
	10½	11½	12	13	13½	13½	in
ARMSCYE DEPTH							
	19	19.5	20.5	21.5	23	24	cm
	7½	7¾	8	8½	9	9½	in
TOTAL LENGTH							
	45.5	48.5	51	54.5	57.5	58.5	cm
	18	19¼	20	21½	22½	23	in
NECK CIRCUMFERENCE							
	21.5	22	23	24	25.5	26.5	cm
	8½	8¾	9	9½	10	10½	in
UPPER ARM CIRCUMFERENCE							
	32	33	34.5	37	38	40.5	cm
	12½	13	13½	14½	15	16	in
LOWER ARM CIRCUMFERENCE BEFORE CUFF DECREASES							
	22	22	22	22	22	22	cm
	8¾	8¾	8¾	8¾	8¾	8¾	in
SLEEVE LENGTH UNDERARM TO CUFF							
	42	42	43	43	46	48	cm
	16½	16½	17	17	18	19	in

SCHEMATIC

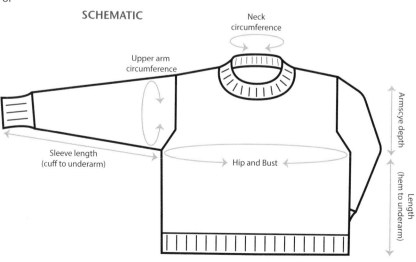

Neck circumference

Upper arm circumference

Sleeve length (cuff to underarm)

Hip and Bust

Armscye depth

Length (hem to underarm)

PATTERN NOTES

This openwork jumper is worked in four shades, with 1x1 ribbing at the hem, cuffs and neckline. The horseshoe lace chart is worked in the round to the underarms, back and forth for front and back, and in the round again for the sleeves. Sleeves are slightly set in, picked up, and worked downwards, reversing the colour / chart sequence to match the body. Where only one number is given this applies to all sizes.

CHART NOTES

Working in the round: Read all rows as right side rows from right to left.

Working flat in rows: Read right side (odd number) rows from right to left, and wrong side (even number) rows from left to right.

SPECIAL TECHNIQUES

Shaping in lace pattern

To keep pattern correct, use the line of k3togtbl from the previous rows to ascertain the position of the repeat. Separate the first and last repeats of the row with stitch markers, then keep track of the decreasing stitch count of each repeat. Check the count at the end of each right side row to ensure that overall stitch count is as expected.

You may also find the following tutorial from our friends at This Is Knit useful:

thisisknit.ie/shaping-in-lace/

ABBREVIATIONS

Standard abbreviations appear on the inside back cover.

INSTRUCTIONS

1

CAST ON, WORK RIB, WORK BODY

With below gauge-size needle and shade A, cast on 280 (300, 320, 340, 380, 420) sts, pm, and join for working in the round.
Round 1: (K1, p1) to end.
Last round sets 1x1 rib.
Place side marker as foll:
Next round: Work 140 (150, 160, 170, 190, 210) sts in rib, pm, work rib to end.
Work in 1x1 rib until piece measure 5cm / 2in from cast-on edge.
Break off A, change to gauge-size needle and B.

Commence working from body chart round 1. Following horseshoe pattern and changing shades where indicated, work from chart until piece measures 26.5 (29, 30.5, 33, 34.5, 34.5) cm / 10½ (11½, 12, 13, 13½, 13½) in from cast-on edge, *or desired length to underarm*, ending with an even-numbered round.

Moving sts around needle without knitting, sl 8 (8, 10, 12, 14, 16) sts each side of each marker to waste yarn. *16 (16, 20, 24, 28, 32) sts set aside at each underarm; 248 (268, 280, 292, 324, 356) sts total with 124 (134, 140, 146, 162, 178) sts rem for front and back.*
Front and back are now separated and you will be working the upper body back and forth in rows.

2

WORK BACK

Keeping chart pattern correct as est, with RS facing, rejoin yarn to back sts and shape armscye as foll:
Step X: K1, ssk, work to last 3 sts, k2tog, k1. *2 sts dec.*
Step Y: P1, p2tog, work to last 3 sts, lld, p1. *2 sts dec.*
Rep steps X and Y a further 2 (3, 4, 3, 4, 3) times. *12 (16, 20, 16, 20, 16) sts dec; 112 (118, 120, 130, 142, 162) sts rem.*

KEY

☐ k on RS, p on WS in shade indicated

■ A: Moonlight

☐ B: Silver

☐ C: Water

■ D: Slate

▨ k3togtbl in shade indicated

◙ yarn over in shade indicated

BODY CHART

29
27
25
23
21
19
17
15
13
11
9
7
5
3
1

10   5   1

SLEEVE CHART

29
27
25
23
21
19
17
15
13
11
9
7
5
3
1

10   5   1

Continue working from chart as est until piece measures 19 (19.5, 20.5, 21.5, 23, 24) cm / 7½ (7¾, 8, 8½, 9, 9½) in from underarm, ending with a WS row.
Moving sts around needle without knitting sl 28 (31, 31, 35, 41, 49) sts to waste yarn for shoulder, then sl 56 (56, 58, 60, 60, 64) sts to a second length of waste yarn for back neck, and finally sl 28 (31, 31, 35, 41, 49) sts to a third length of waste yarn for shoulder.

3 WORK FRONT

Keeping chart pattern correct as est, with RS facing, rejoin yarn to front sts and shape armscye as foll:
Step X: K1, ssk, work to last 3 sts k2tog, k1. *2 sts dec.*
Step Y: P1, p2tog, work to last 3 sts, lld, p1. *2 sts dec.*
Rep steps X and Y a further 2 (3, 4, 3, 4, 3) times. *12 (16, 20, 16, 20, 16) sts dec; 112 (118, 120, 130, 142, 162) sts rem.*

Continue working as est until piece measures 11.5 (12, 12.5, 14, 15, 16.5) cm / 4½ (4¾, 5, 5½, 6, 6½) in from underarm, ending with a WS row. Do not break yarn.
Moving sts around needle without knitting, sl 36 (39, 40, 45, 51, 61) sts for left front, then sl 40 sts to waste yarn and finally sl 36 (39, 40, 45, 51, 61) sts for right front to a spare needle. You will now work each side of the neck separately.

4 WORK LEFT FRONT NECK

Keeping pattern correct as est, shape left front neck as foll:
Step X: Work to last 2 sts, ssk. *1 st dec.*
Step Y: lld, work to end. *1 st dec.*
Rep steps X and Y a further 3 (3, 3, 4, 4, 5) times.
Third size only: work step X once more, then work one further WS row without shaping.
8 (8, 9, 10, 10, 12) sts dec; 28 (31, 31, 35, 41, 49) sts rem.
Continue working as est until left front from underarm measures 19 (19.5, 20.5, 21.5, 23, 24) cm / 7½ (7¾, 8, 8½, 9, 9½) in and matches back. Sl 28 (31, 31, 35, 41, 49) sts to waste yarn for shoulder.

5 WORK RIGHT FRONT NECK

With RS facing, rejoin yarn to right front sts and, keeping pattern correct as est, shape right front neck as foll:
Step X: K2tog, work to end. *1 st dec.*
Step Y: Work to last 2 sts, p2tog. *1 st dec.*
Rep steps X and Y a further 3 (3, 3, 4, 4, 5) times.
Third size only: work step X once more, then work one further WS row without shaping.
8 (8, 9, 10, 10, 12) sts dec; 28 (31, 31, 35, 41, 49) sts rem.
Continue working as est until right front from underarm measures 19 (19.5, 20.5, 21.5, 23, 24) cm / 7½ (7¾, 8, 8½, 9, 9½) in and matches back. Sl 28 (31, 31, 35, 41, 49) sts to waste yarn for shoulder.

6 JOIN SHOULDERS

Using relevant matching shade and gauge-size needle, turn garment inside out and, working 3-needle bind off *from the WS*, join two sets of 28 (31, 31, 35, 41, 49) sts at shoulders.

7 SLEEVES

With A and gauge-size needle(s) of your preferred type for working small circumferences, pick up sts for sleeves as foll: sl 8 (8, 10, 12, 14, 16) sts from waste yarn to needle and k across them; puk 42 (44, 44, 46, 46, 48) sts up armscye to shoulder; puk 42 (44, 44, 46, 46, 48) sts down armscye to underarm, sl 8 (8, 10, 12, 14, 16) sts from waste yarn to needle and k across them, pm for start of round. *100 (104, 108, 116, 120, 128) sts.*

Beginning with *round 2* of sleeve chart, keeping pattern correct, work 10 rounds.
Commence sleeve shaping as foll:
Step X: K1, k2tog, work to last 3 sts, ssk, k1. *2 sts dec.*
Step Y: Work 6 (5, 5, 4, 4, 3) rounds.
Rep steps X and Y a further 14 (16, 18, 22, 24, 28) times. *70 sts rem.*

Continue in pattern as est until sleeve measures 34.5 (34.5, 35.5, 35.5, 38, 40.5) cm / 13½ (13½, 14, 14, 15, 16) in (*or desired length minus 7.5cm / 3in*) from underarm ending with chart round 10, 20 or 30.

8 CUFFS

Change to A and k 1 round, decreasing 18 (18, 16, 14, 14, 14) sts evenly across round. *52 (52, 54, 56, 56, 56) sts.*
Change to below gauge-size needle and work in 1x1 rib, as est for body, for 7.5cm / 3in.
Bind off loosely in rib.

Rep steps 7 & 8 for second sleeve.

9 NECKBAND

With A, and below gauge-size needles, starting at **right** back neck, sl 56 (56, 58, 60, 60, 64) back neck sts from waste yarn to needle and k across them; puk 22 sts down left front neck, sl 40 front sts from waste yarn to needle and k across them, puk 22 sts up right front neck, pm, and join for working in the round. *140 (140, 142, 144, 144, 148) sts.*

Commence working 1x1 rib, decreasing 14 sts evenly across the first round. *126 (126, 128, 130, 130, 134) sts rem.*
Continue to work in 1x1 rib, as est for body, until neckband measures 4cm / 1½in.
Bind off in rib.

10 FINISHING

Weave in all ends to the back of the work. Soak garment in cool water for at least 20 minutes, shape to dimensions given in sizing table, pin out, block flat and leave to dry completely. Take care not to overstretch the lace (that is, don't stretch or block vigorously, as you might with a shawl).

Enjoy your Myrtle sweater!

ALTNAFEADH

I t's time to climb the Devil's Staircase. The name certainly has a fearful ring. You cross the road at Altnafeadh, location of one of the most photographed houses in Scotland, standing quietly in the shadow of Buachaille Etive Mòr. Altnafeadh was once a stance for droving traffic, but in recent years climbers have taken the place of cattle, overnighting here before they make an attempt on the Buachaille's granite buttresses. With these mighty mountains behind you and Glencoe's dark valley off to the side, the landscape seems, in many ways, intimidating. Will the Devil's Staircase live up to its name?

You cross a small footbridge and begin your ascent. The view behind you, down the glen, grows perhaps even more impressive as you climb, and the path in front of you seems well laid out and rather inviting: cutting its neat course up the hillside, twisting this way and that. If you are walking the Devil's Staircase in summer, you might find the going rather jolly, with groups of West Highland Way-ers moving steadily up the zigzags together, and cheery chalk-daubed signs announcing the remaining distance to the tented "tuck shop" where you might choose to refresh yourself with a welcome can of Irn Bru. The views are something to drink in, too. Behind you, the dramatic curve of Glencoe; before you, the elegant peaks of the Mamores. If you'd like a first sight of Ben Nevis, you could take a detour here, climbing the sharp ridge westwards to the top of Stob Mhic Mhartuin. But here, at the summit of the Devil's Staircase, the views are certainly spectacular enough. At 550 metres, this is the highest point of the West Highland Way, but getting up here was not terribly difficult after all. So, what has the devil got to do with it?

Though commonly understood to refer to the physical demands of the path on the walking body, this is not the case. The Devil's Staircase is so called because constructing it was a devil of a job, and it was named thus by the eighteenth-century English soldiers who built it. After the 1715 Jacobite Rising, the British government constructed huge forts and garrisons in the Scottish Highlands. Soldiers were stationed, armed and ready to repress any Stuart-supporting rebellion, but movement between their military outposts proved difficult over the rough Highland terrain. In 1725, General George Wade was appointed *Commander-in-Chief of His Majesty's Forces, Castles, Forts and Barracks in North Britain* (i.e. Scotland), and began the ambitious scheme of military road-building that was to transform the Highland landscape.

The difficulty of travel by foot, horse or carriage north of the Border had become notorious: "the old ways (for roads I shall not call them)", wrote one of Wade's officers, Edmund Burt, "consisted chiefly of stony moors, bogs, rugged rapid fords, declivities of hills, entangling woods and giddy precipices. You will say that this is a dreadful catalogue to be read to him that is about to take a highland journey."

Wade's roads opened up the landscape, allowing easy travel between locales which, because they were divided by huge lochs, deep glens and high passes, had previously been regarded as impossibly remote. His new roads heralded a modern era of accessibility, connection and communication in the Highlands, but their ultimate purpose was, of course, the control and repression of both the landscape and its people. Michael Pollard neatly summarises the meaning and purpose of the roads of Wade and his successors as effective "instruments of a colonial regime". If one were in any doubt about the roads' actual and symbolic function, consider the encomium to General Wade in the controversial sixth verse of the patriotic eighteenth-century song that was to become Britain's national anthem:

> *God grant that Marshal Wade*
> *May by Thy mighty aid*
> *Victory bring.*
> *May he sedition hush*
> *And like a torrent rush*
> *Rebellious Scots to crush -*
> *God save the King!*

In 1732, Wade passed the management of the road-building programme on to his successor, William Caulfeild. After the 1745 Rising, Caulfeild set out to link Stirling to Fort William with a road which covers much of the route followed by today's West Highland Way from Tyndrum to Inveroran and over Rannoch

Moor. At Kingshouse (then used as a garrison), Caulfeild faced a choice. Should his road head on to Fort William by turning west, down Glencoe? This route was simpler, but much longer, and its continuity was broken up by the waters of Loch Leven, where a ferry crossing would be necessary. Or should he take a more direct but much more difficult route by turning north, up the steep hill opposite Altnafeadh, crossing down through the Mamores before making the final descent to the fort? Faced with such dilemmas, Caulfeild was generally inclined to take the easier course of action, but in this case he decided on the more direct route. His reports suggest that he'd planned his zigzagging path up the hillside – carefully skirting the ridge of the Aonach Eagach and the head of Loch Leven – by 1750. Work to build the Devil's Staircase began.

Caulfeild's construction season was between May and October, and up to 500 men were involved, working in parties of around 100, with each group headed up by officers. Sleeping in tents out on the moor and living on a spartan diet of oatmeal and cheese, working soldiers received sixpence for every day that they spent hacking out the hillside to create the Devil's Staircase. The weather was often inclement, and when work had to stop, the men might face days of enforced idleness with no pay. Breaking their way steadily through the rock and peat, Caulfeild's men laboured with their hand-held picks, digging out the path, introducing drainage routes and laying down a surface of stony cobbles. When one pictures the intense, back-breaking labour that went into carving out these steep zigzags up the hillside, it comes as no surprise that the men who toiled here might refer to it as the devil's work.

AN ICON OF SCOTTISH OPEN ACCESS
By the time that the British government construction programme reached its peak in 1767, Wade and Caulfeild's network of military roads covered almost 1,000 miles. There were almost 1,000 bridges too, over which countless thousands of feet would tramp in the coming decades, across the Highlands. One of those pairs of feet belonged to S. T. Coleridge, who was evidently impressed by the scale and extent of the sixteen-foot-wide road Caulfeild's men had cut through the landscape. "Walked a brisk pace under the inspiration of a bottle of Burton's ale from Tyndrum to Inveroran," Coleridge recorded in his notebook: "a fine road." Crossing Rannoch Moor, Coleridge compared the high quality of Caulfeild's route to what he regarded the poverty of his surroundings. While he had nothing positive to say about the moor, he was deeply impressed by Caulfeild's "beautiful road such as you may see in noblemen's pleasure grounds".

Ironically, Caulfeild's successors decided that there were much easier ways to get to and from Fort William than over the Devil's Staircase. By 1785, a more straightforward path through Glencoe to the Ballachulish ferry had been introduced, following much of the route of what was later to become the A82 trunk road. But the Devil's Staircase achieved almost immediate

notoriety as a tourist landmark. Travelling up the glen on a peat cart in 1799, intrepid Sarah Murray carefully ticked off the Devil's Staircase from her list of essential Glencoe sights to see. "This dreadfully steep zig-zag up the front of a mountain," Murray remarked, astonished: "I cannot conceive how any sort of wheel carriage could ever go up and down it, or even the shelties keep upon their legs." The Devil's Staircase was now one of the many features of the dark glen at which romantic visitors might shudder in consternation.

Today, there is little that is devilish about the Devil's Staircase. And perhaps it is ironic that this former symbol of imperial control has now become an icon of Scottish open access. Today, the Devil's Staircase grants thousands of West Highland Way walkers unfettered passage through the hills, enabling them to enjoy some fine high-level walking, and truly spectacular Highland views. ☺☺

ALTNAFEADH

Long elegant gauntlets, with a zigzagging structure (just like the Devil's Staircase).

YARN
Fyberspates Cumulus (74% baby suri alpaca; 26% silk; 150m / 164yds per 25g ball)
A: Indigo; 1 x 25g ball
B: Raindrop; 1 x 25g ball
C: Thistle; 1 x 25g ball
D: Ethereal; 1 x 25g ball

NEEDLES AND NOTIONS
Gauge-size and below gauge-size needle(s) of your preferred type for working small circumferences.
Tapestry needle.

GAUGE
32 sts and 38 rounds to 10cm / 4in over horseshoe lace pattern using gauge-size needle(s).
Gauge was achieved with 2.75mm / US 2 needle.

SIZE
To fit hand: 18-20.5cm / 7-8in circumference (at palm)
Finished length: 41.5cm / 16¼in
Finished circumference (below wrist): 16cm / 6¼in
Note: Lace and rib pattern is very stretchy: gauntlets should fit most adult hands.

ABBREVIATIONS
Standard abbreviations appear on the inside back cover.

PATTERN NOTES
Combining 1x1 rib with graphic horseshoe lace, these gauntlets are worked from the bottom up. Starting with a stretchy cast-on, a few rounds of rib are worked, followed by several repeats of the four-shade horseshoe lace pattern. Working the wrist on a below gauge-size needle ensures the lace fits snugly, before the hand and thumb opening are added in 1x1 rib.

INSTRUCTIONS

1

CAST ON, WORK CUFF

With below gauge-size needle(s) and shade D, cast on 75 sts, pm, and join for working in the round.
Change to A and knit 1 round.
Set-up round: (K2tog, p1) 25 times. *25 sts dec; 50 sts rem.*
Next round: (K1, p1) to end.
Last round sets 1x1 rib.
Work a further 9 rounds in 1x1 rib.

2

WORK LACE

Change to gauge-size needle(s), join in B, and work from chart as foll:
Changing shades as indicated, work chart rounds 1-30 twice, then chart rounds 1-18 once more.
Change to below gauge-size needle and work chart rounds 19-30.

3

CREATE THUMB OPENING, WORK GAUNTLET TOP

With below gauge-size needle(s) and A, knit 1 round decreasing 6 sts evenly across round. *6 sts dec; 44 sts rem.*
Work 12 rounds in 1x1 rib as est for cuff.
Remove marker, turn work, and, keeping 1x1 rib correct, commence working across sts back and forth in rows (rather than in the round) to create thumb opening as foll:
Row 1 (WS): (K1, p1) to end.
Row 2 (RS): (K1, p1) to end.
Work a further 13 rows in 1x1 rib, ending with a WS row.
Turn work so RS is facing, and recommence working in the round again as foll:
Next round: Replace marker, keeping 1x1 rib in the round correct, work across all sts.
Work a further 26 rounds in 1x1 rib.
With D, bind off in rib.

4

FINISH THUMB OPENING

With below gauge-size needle and D, puk 24 sts evenly around thumb-opening.
On next round, bind off all 24 sts.

5

FINISHING

Weave in all ends to the back of the work. Soak gauntlets in cool water for 20 mins. Press dry between towels and shape to dimensions given. Block over glove blockers if you have them, or pin out. Leave to dry completely.

Enjoy your Altnafeadh gauntlets!

BODY CHART

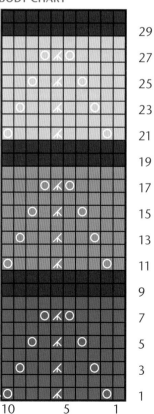

KEY

■ A: Indigo, k

■ B: Raindrop, k

▨ C: Thistle, k

□ D: Ethereal, k

▨ k3togtbl in shade indicated

 yarn over in shade indicated

ELECTRIC VILLAGE

At the close of the nineteenth century, aluminium was regarded as a symbol of the future. More rare and precious than either gold or platinum, aluminium's low density, resistance to corrosion and high conductivity meant it carried an obvious (and enormous) commercial potential. All over the world, industrial pioneers competed to exploit this quintessentially modern metal, but the enigmatic material was enormously difficult to produce. Electrolysis was costly and involved, and new methods of furnace extraction demanded vast quantities of cheap power. At the dawn of the new century, the British Aluminium Company decided that the solution to their very modern problem lay in the ancient landscape of the Scottish Highlands. To generate the vast quantity of electricity necessary for efficient aluminium-smelting, they would exploit the West Highlands' much-underused resource: water. In the decades that followed, ambitious hydroelectric schemes, large-scale aluminium manufacturing and the unlikely hub of Britain's first "electric village" radically transformed the quiet landscape of Lochaber.

In the mountains high above the site the company had earmarked as their manufacturing base, a chain of lochs drained westwards from Rannoch Moor to Loch Leven and the coast. The Blackwater River would need to be dammed and its water redirected. From the hilltop reservoir, planned at a height of more than 1,000 feet, water would plunge down into the glen at a force capable of generating more than 2,000 kiloWatts of power. Plans were drawn up, and the call for labour was answered by men from central Scotland, the Gaelic-speaking Western Isles and across the Irish Sea. Poorly paid and badly treated, when they weren't hacking rock from the hillside, these navvies endured terrible conditions in a cold and lawless shanty town. Dermod Flynn, the narrator of Patrick MacGill's autobiographical memoir of the Blackwater dam, recalls his first sight of the accommodation:

"A sleepy hollow lay below; and within it a muddle of shacks, roofed with tarred canvas, and built of driven piles were huddled together in bewildering confusion. These were surrounded by puddles, heaps of disused wood, tins, bottles and all manner of discarded rubbish. Some of the shacks had windows, most of them had none; everything was in a most haphazard condition and it looked as if the buildings had dropped out of the sky by accident and were just allowed to remain where they had fallen."

The work was hard and the conditions truly brutal: "over an area of two square miles thousands of men laboured, some on the day shift, some on the night shift, some engaged on blasting operations, some wheeling muck and others building dams and hewing rock facings". MacGill's writing powerfully conveys the alienation of the navvies from the final outcome of their work. They were "despised men" lifting rock and pouring concrete with no knowledge of electricity or aluminium:

"We never asked questions concerning the ultimate issue of our labours ... There were so many tons of earth to be lifted and thrown somewhere else; we lifted them and threw them somewhere else; so many cubic yards of iron-hard rocks to be blasted and carried away: we blasted and carried them away."

In just five years, MacGill and his 3,000 fellow workers built the extraordinary structure whose huge sweep is visible from many of the surrounding summits of Lochaber and Glencoe. To create the dam, the reservoir and the innovative roofed conduits which brought the water down the mountain, 50,000 tons of concrete had been carried up into the hills. Countless men died in the construction of Blackwater – and a poignant reminder of their labours is offered by a tiny mountain graveyard with twenty-two headstones, many simply marked "unknown".

A MODERN COMMUNITY

Meanwhile, down in the glen, work was under way on the new aluminium factory. The output generated by the Blackwater scheme vastly exceeded that of any British hydroelectric plant then in existence: more than enough to power the smelter's huge Pelton turbines. And where the navvies' shanty town had stood, the company began to build a bright, new, modern village to house its workers. Construction was only permitted on one side of the river – and here, in the shadow of the surrounding mountains, the new houses would lie in darkness during the four long winter months. But, though the village had little natural daylight, it would benefit enormously from artificial illumination.

From public streetlamps to private homes, Lochaber's new "electric village" was to receive free lighting courtesy of the aluminium company. At the time of the village's development, the majority of Britain was illuminated by gas – and, without the standardisation of a national grid, electricity remained a luxury enjoyed only by the rich. Yet, when London was still gaslit, a tiny community in Lochaber found itself at the cutting edge of modern technology. "Aluminiumville" was proposed as a name for the new electric village, but "Kinlochleven" was settled on instead.

When the factory began its official operation in 1909, global demand for aluminium was fairly low, and the company faced the threat of overproduction. But the First World War heralded an aluminium boom, as the metal was increasingly needed for the development of aircraft and modern weaponry. When the men of the electric village were conscripted, and left home for the trenches, the women of Kinlochleven filled their jobs. Women drove supply trucks, worked at the furnace and operated the electric trams which carried thousands of tons of aluminium to Ballachulish and the barges waiting at the wharves. As demand for the new metal continued to grow, the aluminium company expanded its Lochaber operations. Further smelting plants were built, with associated infrastructure taking on the challenges of the Highland landscape, including fifteen miles of pressure tunnel which had to be driven through the bedrock of Ben Nevis. The labour of German prisoners-of-war was exploited alongside that of Scottish and Irish navvies deemed incapable of active service. Together these men built a beautiful new road out of Kinlochleven, curving around the mountains and lochside to Glencoe.

FROM ALUMINIUM TO RENEWABLE ENERGY

By the 1920s, the employment opportunities and modern amenities of the electric village meant that it remained largely immune to the inter-war depression that affected Scotland's cities. The village cinema got "talkies" around the same time as Edinburgh, and busloads of visitors would arrive in Kinlochleven from miles around to enjoy its modern films and dances. Here, in the middle of Lochaber, was a jazz-age settlement with its face proudly turned towards the future. Women still worked in "men's" jobs, together with large numbers of displaced Europeans – and this diverse workforce brought a liberal, cosmopolitan atmosphere to the electric village. Good working conditions, locally focused education and research programmes and numerous other benefits provided by the company in what was, effectively, a mini-welfare state, made Kinlochleven a thriving, vibrant and highly progressive rural community.

But the good times of the electric village did not last forever. After the Second World War, Russia and China joined the rush towards aluminium, technology moved on apace – and, from being a cutting-edge, modern manufacturer, the Kinlochleven smelter became one of the world's oldest and smallest. Company buy-outs, economies of scale and out-of-date technology meant that the smelter was finally forced to cease production in 1994. For a community which had been built with the sole purpose of making aluminium, and which had remained, for almost a century, entirely dependent on this single industry and the employment it provided, the effect was completely devastating. In recent years, visitors (such as those walking the West Highland Way) have provided a much-

needed boost to the economy of Kinlochleven (if you stay in the Blackwater Hostel, you'll be occupying the aluminium company's former research laboratory).

Yet the story of the electric village has recently come full circle. In 2017, following years of research, infrastructure redevelopment, new construction and £13 million of investment, a new hydroelectric power station was finally switched on in Kinlochleven. Rather than industrial manufacturing, this time the scheme's sole purpose is the generation of "green" electricity; and ring-fenced funding drawn from profits will benefit the whole community. As a twenty-first-century producer of renewable energy, the electric village continues to regenerate itself. ◉◉

ELECTRIC VILLAGE

A dramatic, graphic wrap.

YARN
Fyberspates Cumulus (74% baby suri alpaca; 26% silk; 150m / 164yds per 25g ball)
A: Plum; 3 x 25g balls
B: Onyx; 2 x 25g balls
C: Pearl; 2 x 25g balls

NEEDLES AND NOTIONS
Gauge-size needle(s) of your preferred type / length.
Stitch markers (if required) for separating pattern repeats and slipped st edging.
Tapestry needle.

GAUGE
20 sts and 24 rows (12 ridges) to 10cm / 4in over chevron stripe pattern using gauge-size needle.
Gauge was achieved with 3.75mm / US 5 needle.
Gauge is not crucial in this pattern, but bear in mind that differences may significantly affect yarn quantities and finished size of hap.

SIZE
Finished length: 229cm / 90in
Finished width at widest point: 89cm / 35in

SPECIAL TECHNIQUES
MPSS bind-off – see Special Techniques section on page 126.

Dealing with shade changes over striped sections:
Carry the yarn not in use loosely up the side of the work.

PATTERN NOTES
A few stitches are cast on, the neat slipped stitch edging is established, and plain and chevron stripe sections are worked alternately in the hap's 3 different shades. Increases are progressively incorporated into one long side of each section to create a dramatic hap with a large triangular shape. After working a couple of sections without shaping, the hap concludes with a final chevron-stripe flourish.

SCHEMATIC

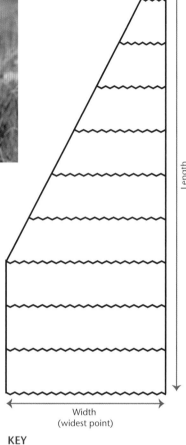

Length

Width
(widest point)

CHART NOTES

Read right side (odd number) rows from right to left, and
wrong side (even number) rows from left to right.

ABBREVIATIONS

Standard abbreviations appear on the inside back cover.

CHART X

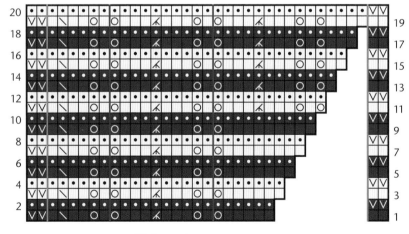

10 st repeat

CHART Y

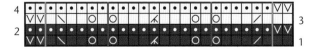

10 st repeat

KEY

☐	k on RS, p on WS in shade indicated
⊡	p on RS, k on WS in shade indicated
☐	B: Pearl
■	C: Onyx
⊙	yarn over in shade indicated
◪	k3tog in shade indicated
⧄	k2tog in shade indicated
◣	ssk in shade indicated
⋁	sl1pwise wyif in shade indicated
⎮	edging marker (optional)
❙	pattern repeat

INSTRUCTIONS

1

SET UP EDGE AND CENTRE PATTERN

With shade A and gauge-size needle, cast on
5 sts.
Set up (RS): K3, sl2 pwise wyif.
Set up (WS): K3, sl2 pwise wyif.

2

ESTABLISH PLAIN SECTION

With A, increase sts over next 6 rows as foll:
Row 1 (RS)(inc): K2, kfb, k to last 2 sts, sl2 pwise wyif. *1 st inc.*
Row 2 (WS): K to last 2 sts, sl2 pwise wyif.
Row 3 (inc): K2, kfb, k to last 2 sts, sl2 pwise wyif. *1 st inc.*
Rows 4-6: K to last 2 sts, sl2 pwise wyif.
This pattern (increasing on the first and third row of every 6-row repeat) is repeated throughout each plain section.
Rep rows 1-6 a further 9 times. *60 rows worked; 20 sts inc; 25 sts.*

3

ESTABLISH CHEVRON STRIPE SECTION

Break off A, join in B, and establish chevron stripe pattern and increases as foll referring to written instructions below, or reading from chart X:
Row 1 (RS)(inc): With B, k7, yo, *k1, yo, k3, k3tog, k3, yo; rep from * to last 8 sts, k1, yo, k2, ssk, k1, sl2 pwise wyif.
Row 2 (and all foll WS rows): K to last 2 sts, sl2 pwise wyif.
Join in C.
Row 3 (inc): With C, k8, yo, *k1, yo, k3, k3tog, k3, yo; rep from * to last 8 sts, k1, yo, k2, ssk, k1, sl2 pwise wyif.
Row 5 (inc): With B, k9, yo, *k1, yo, k3, k3tog, k3, yo; rep from * to last 8 sts, k1, yo, k2, ssk, k1, sl2 pwise wyif.
Row 7 (inc): With C, k10, yo, *k1, yo, k3, k3tog, k3, yo; rep from * to last 8 sts, k1, yo, k2, ssk, k1, sl2 pwise wyif.
Row 9 (inc): With B, k11, yo, *k1, yo, k3, k3tog, k3, yo; rep from * to last 8 sts, k1, yo, k2, ssk, k1, sl2 pwise wyif.

Row 11 (inc): With C, k2, yo, *k1, yo, k3, k3tog, k3, yo; rep from * to last 8 sts, k1, yo, k2, ssk, k1, sl2 pwise wyif.
Row 13 (inc): With B, k3, yo, *k1, yo, k3, k3tog, k3, yo; rep from * to last 8 sts, k1, yo, k2, ssk, k1, sl2 pwise wyif.
Row 15 (inc): With C, k4, yo, *k1, yo, k3, k3tog, k3, yo; rep from * to last 8 sts, k1, yo, k2, ssk, k1, sl2 pwise wyif.
Row 17 (inc): With B, k5, yo, *k1, yo, k3, k3tog, k3, yo; rep from * to last 8 sts, k1, yo, k2, ssk, k1, sl2 pwise wyif.
Row 19 (inc): With C, k6, yo, *k1, yo, k3, k3tog, k3, yo; rep from * to last 8 sts, k1, yo, k2, ssk, k1, sl2 pwise wyif.
Row 20 (WS): As row 2.
Last 20 rows set chevron-stripe and increase pattern and are repeated throughout each stripe section. Another 10-st bracketed repeat is added every 20 rows.

Rep chevron-stripe and increase pattern rows 1-20 twice more. *60 pattern rows worked; 30 sts inc; 55 sts.*

4

REPEAT PLAIN AND CHEVRON STRIPE SECTIONS

Rep steps 2 and 3 twice more, increasing and incorporating additional pattern repeats as est. *100 sts inc; 155 sts.*

5

WORK PLAIN SECTION

Row 1 (RS)(inc): With A, K2, kfb, k to last 2 sts, sl2 pwise wyif. *1 st inc.*
Row 2 (WS): K to last 2 sts, sl2 pwise wyif.
Row 3 (inc): K2, kfb, k to last 2 sts, sl2 pwise wyif. *1 st inc.*
Row 4-6: K to last 2 sts, sl2 pwise wyif.
Rep rows 1-6 a further 8 times, then work rows 1-4 only once more.
Next row (inc): K2, kfb, k to last 2 sts, sl2 pwise wyif.
Next row: K to last 2 sts, sl2 pwise wyif.
21 sts inc; 176 sts.

6

WORK NO-INCREASE STRIPE SECTION

Referring to chart Y or foll written instructions below, work 4-row chevron stripe pattern *without* increasing as foll:
Row 1 (RS): With B, k3, k2tog, k3, yo, *k1, yo, k3, k3tog, k3, yo; rep from * to last 8 sts, k1, yo, k2, ssk, k1, sl2 pwise wyif.
Row 2 (WS): With B, k to last 2 sts, sl2 pwise wyif.
Row 3: With C, as row 1.
Row 4: With C, as row 2.
Changing shades and keeping slipped st edging correct as est, rep rows 1-4 a further 29 times. *60 straight rows worked.*

7

WORK NO-INCREASE PLAIN SECTION

With A, keeping garter st and slipped st edging pattern correct as est, work 60 plain rows *without shaping.*

8

WORK FINAL NO-INCREASE STRIPE SECTION

Rep step 6. *60 striped rows worked.*
Bind off using MPSS stretchy bind-off (see special techniques), or your preferred stretchy method.

9

FINISHING

Weave in all ends to the back of the work.
Soak wrap in cool water for 20 mins. Press dry between towels and, with blocking wires and pins, stretch and shape to dimensions given. Leave to dry completely.

Enjoy your Electric Village wrap!

THE
OBSERVATORY

If you make it all the way to the top of Britain's highest mountain, you are unlikely to see the sun, for this craggy ruin of a Devonian volcano is cloud-covered on five days out of six. Here, 4,411 feet above sea level, it's chilly too. You'll experience temperatures that are close to or below zero, and always around 8° cooler than the base of the mountain in Fort William. And, if you turn your face to the sky, you'll probably feel rain or snow in the air, since, depending the time of year, the near-continuous precipitation rate on the summit plateau can range from 1 to 6 inches daily. The meteorological data for the summit of this mountain is unusually rich and comprehensive. That's because a group of visionary Victorians decided to use Ben Nevis to carefully study that most British of topics: the weather.

Two British meteorological societies were established in the mid-nineteenth century: the English one in 1850 and its Scottish counterpart in 1855. Both were, from their inception, energetic and ambitious groups, in which large numbers of dedicated weather-watchers all over Britain shared their findings with alacrity. The British climate is at the mercy of Atlantic weather systems, and it was increasingly thought that mountain-top observation might be the best way to study their effects. In 1877, a proposal was made to build a meteorological observatory on the summit plateau of Ben Nevis. Grant requests were submitted to the government, but the proposals were turned down. With empty pockets, the meteorologists were forced to abandon their ambitious mountain-top study plans.

But the Ben Nevis observatory project was to receive a huge boost from an energetic amateur, Clement Wragge. Flamboyant, eccentric and independently wealthy, Wragge took it upon himself to personally demonstrate the irrefutable usefulness of the meteorological data that the summit of Ben Nevis might provide. So, he moved his family to Fort William and embarked upon an extraordinary data-collection scheme. On June 1st, 1881, Wragge arose at 4:30am and, accompanied by his trusty Newfoundland dog, Renzo, began an ascent of the mountain. At 7am he paused, to take his first set of readings by the lochan at Meall an t-Suidhe, noting the barometric pressure, wind direction and strength, the air temperature

and humidity. Reaching the top of Ben Nevis by 9am, he spent two hours on the summit carrying out observations at thirty-minute intervals, then carefully conducted further timed readings during the full course of his long descent. Meanwhile, back home in Fort William, Wragge's wife, Leonore, had spent her day making meteorological observations at comparable intervals to her husband. Working together in this fashion, the Wragges created two comparable meteorological datasets from 33 and 4,411 feet. The next day, Clement Wragge got up at the same time and repeated his ascent. Then he did it again. And again. He climbed Ben Nevis almost every day, in fact, until October 13th, when, after discovering that a storm had destroyed the roof of the caged structure in which he housed his instruments, he was forced to abandon his experiment.

WEATHER AND WONDER

By anybody's standards, what Wragge accomplished that summer was extraordinary. Rising and climbing up the mountain whatever the weather, Wragge was indefatigable in his efforts – and the sight of the familiar wind-battered sodden figure struggling off the Ben soon drew him the local nickname of "Inclement Rag". At the summit, Wragge often had to light a fire in order to warm his fingers for movement sufficient to conduct his observations – and, during those nineteen long, tiring weeks, he endured every meteorological excess that the mountain could muster. Wragge's remarkable dedication to his cause began to draw attention, and in late August he was joined in his daily labours by a reporter from the London *Times*. Struggling upwards in horizontal sleet and a Force 11 gale, the two men made their way across the summit plateau like Renzo, on all fours, so that Wragge could finally take his readings. The journalist's report of this treacherous ascent created an instant sensation. Vivid accounts of Wragge's work on Ben Nevis captured the public imagination: he rapidly became a household name, and in a way his work was done.

The following year, a crowdfunding appeal was launched to build a Ben Nevis observatory, and donations began to pour in immediately from all over the country. Within weeks, more than £4,000 had been raised, Wragge was awarded a Scottish Meteorological Society gold medal, and construction work had commenced.

Working at impressive speed, in just four months, local Lochaber labourers built the bridle path which enabled the observatory's construction materials to be carried up the mountain. The most important thing about the structure was its weatherproofing: the building was double-skinned and double-glazed, with a wooden core encased in a thick stone shell that would withstand the winter gales. Nine months' worth of non-perishable food was placed in the observatory larder (in the likely event of the delivery of fresh supplies being delayed) – and a maritime cable, similar to that used for the first transatlantic telegraph, was laid down to enable contact between the observatory and Fort William.

On October 17th, 1883, Mrs Cameron Campbell (the then owner of the Ben Nevis estate) left Fort William with great fanfare and made her way up the bridleway on a pony, alongside several meteorologists. At the summit, she was handed the keys to the observatory, and, after an appropriate pause for tea, declared the building open. Staff moved in, and regular observations commenced that November. From the beginning, the Ben Nevis weathermen faced tremendous difficulties in their work. Since it was impossible on a bare summit to measure wind force with the accepted Beaufort scale (which relied on assessing the wind's effects on surrounding objects), the men devised an ingenious method of leaning into gales on the observatory roof, and measuring the angle of their bodies. The summit plateau was encased in thick cloud for 80% of the winter months, in December only a single hour of sunlight was recorded, and it proved impossible to measure precipitation with any degree of accuracy since so much fell as snow. And the snow just kept on coming, drifting and falling and piling itself around the observatory building to a depth of 12 feet or more. In particularly bad weather, it was impossible to dig an access route out from the front door, and the men might find themselves holed up inside the building for days on end.

The mountain conditions the meteorologists had come to study were certainly intense, and they were also often beautiful or bizarre. Official logbooks, as well as the personal diaries of observatory workers, abound with awe-filled accounts of the wild weather of the lonely summit plateau. With unrestrained wonder, the weathermen described their experience of spectacular sunrises and sunsets, inversions, electrical storms, St Elmo's fire, and the beautiful blue, rare noctilucent clouds created by ice crystals at high altitudes. It is no surprise that those drawn to the observatory were already curious about the

environment and the weather; but many went on to develop keen scientific interests in meteorological phenomena, and perhaps none more so than renowned physicist, C. T. R. Wilson.

Wilson worked as a relief observer on Ben Nevis for two weeks in September 1894, and the logbook reveals a period of exceptionally fine weather, with very little precipitation and unusual amounts of sunshine. Wilson enjoyed a blissful anticyclonic fortnight on the summit during which, standing alone with the sun at his back and the clouds beneath his feet, he would frequently observe a Brocken spectre. This optical effect, in which a human shadow is cast, magnified and surrounded by a rainbow-hued refraction of water droplets, intrigued Wilson, as it had intrigued (and continues to intrigue) many of those interested in mountain environments and their aesthetics. Experiencing this unusual phenomenon is something like the ultimate selfie: you can only see your own Brocken spectre (because the sun has to be directly behind you), and the atmosphere itself effectively becomes one huge mirror, reflecting back your disproportionately projected self with its weirdly shimmering rainbow halo.

When he came down off Ben Nevis, Wilson became preoccupied with recreating the conditions in which Brocken spectres might appear. Working at the Cavendish Laboratory in Cambridge, he began to investigate the relationship between optical phenomena and humid air, developing an experimental study environment which he referred to as a cloud chamber. Saturating the air inside the chamber, and then expanding and condensing it, Wilson discovered that ions acted as centres around which water droplets formed. Wilson's vision of his own Brocken spectre while working at the Ben Nevis observatory had inspired the development of his cloud chamber, which eventually detected ionising radiation, which in turn enabled rapid progress to be made in the field of modern particle physics. For the remarkable discoveries and far-reaching influence of the cloud chamber, Wilson was awarded the Nobel Prize for Physics in 1927.

The last logbook entry at the Ben Nevis observatory was produced on October 1st, 1904, a day of heavy snow and cloud. British Government support for Scottish meteorology had not proved forthcoming, and it was impossible to maintain the enterprise through private donation alone. But, during the twenty-one years of its existence, the Ben Nevis observatory had provided one of the most continuous and complete records of mountain meteorology in existence. Its development, construction and two decades of data collection by its dedicated weathermen represent, by any standards, a terrific achievement. The visionary scheme of Clement Wragge and his contemporaries led directly to the construction of other summit observatories, such as on Norway's Haldde Mountain (1899). From beneath the snow-covered rubble on the plateau of Ben Nevis, its story continues to inspire. ⊙⊙

Additional photography: Gordon Anderson

THE
OBSERVATORY

Delicate peaked lace combines with straightforward garter stitch in this elegantly simple hap.

YARN
Fyberspates Cumulus (74% baby suri alpaca; 26% silk; 150m / 164yds per 25g ball)
Pearl; 3 x 25g balls

NEEDLES AND NOTIONS
Gauge-size needle(s) of your preferred type / length.
2 locking stitch markers.
Tapestry needle.

GAUGE
14 sts and 36 rows to 10cm / 4in over garter st using gauge-size needle.
Gauge was achieved with 3.75mm / US 5 needle.
Gauge is not crucial in this pattern, but bear in mind that differences may significantly affect yarn quantities and finished size of hap.

SIZE
Finished width: 168cm / 66in
Finished depth: 46cm / 18in

SPECIAL TECHNIQUES
MPSS bind-off – see Special Techniques section on page 126.

PATTERN NOTES
The lace edging is created first, as one long strip. Stitches are then picked up from the centre of the lace edge, and each row is worked outwards, picking up stitches progressively along the long edge of the lace to create an elegant curved shape. The top edge is finished with a neat stretchy bind off and the whole hap is blocked to size.

CHART NOTES
Read right side (odd number) rows from right to left, and wrong side (even number) rows from left to right.

ABBREVIATIONS
Standard abbreviations appear on the inside back cover.

WRITTEN INSTRUCTIONS

Set-up rows
Row 1 (RS): Yo, ssk, k to end.
Row 2 (WS): Sl1 pwise wyib, k2, (yo, ssk) 5 times, k2, k2tog, yo, k2tog, k1.

Lace pattern
Row 1 (RS and all foll RS rows): Yo, ssk, k to end.
Row 2 (WS): Sl1 pwise wyib, k1, (yo, ssk) 5 times, k3, yo, ssk, yo, k2.
Row 4: Sl1 pwise wyib, k2, (yo, ssk) 4 times, k3, (yo, ssk) twice, yo, k2.
Row 6: Sl1 pwise wyib, k1, (yo, ssk) 4 times, k3, (yo, ssk) 3 times, yo, k2.
Row 8: Sl1 pwise wyib, k2, (yo, ssk) 3 times, k3, (yo, ssk) 4 times, yo, k2.
Row 10: Sl1 pwise wyib, k1, (yo, ssk) 3 times, k3, (yo, ssk) 5 times, yo, k2.
Row 12: Sl1 pwise wyib, k2, (yo, ssk) twice, k3, (yo, ssk) 6 times, yo, k2.
Row 14: Sl1 pwise wyib, k1, (yo, ssk) twice, k3, (yo, ssk) 7 times, yo, k2.
Row 16: Sl1 pwise wyib, k2, (yo, ssk) twice, k2, (k2tog, yo) 7 times, k2tog, k1.
Row 18: Sl1 pwise wyib, k1, (yo, ssk) 3 times, k2, (k2tog, yo) 6 times, k2tog, k1.
Row 20: Sl1 pwise wyib, k2, (yo, ssk) 3 times, k2, (k2tog, yo) 5 times, k2tog, k1.
Row 22: Sl1 pwise wyib, k1, (yo, ssk) 4 times, k2, (k2tog, yo) 4 times, k2tog, k1.
Row 24: Sl1 pwise wyib, k2, (yo, ssk) 4 times, k2, (k2tog, yo) 3 times, k2tog, k1.
Row 26: Sl1 pwise wyib, k1, (yo, ssk) 5 times, k2, (k2tog, yo) twice, k2tog, k1.
Row 28: Sl1 pwise wyib, k2, (yo, ssk) 5 times, k2, k2tog, yo, k2tog, k1.

KEY

⊡ ssk on RS; k2tog on WS

⊡ ssk on WS

⊡ sl1 pwise wyib

⊡ yarn over

□ pattern repeat

1 set up row

NOTE: Pattern is 26 sts at widest point

CHART

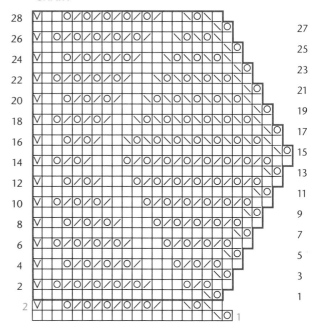

SCHEMATIC

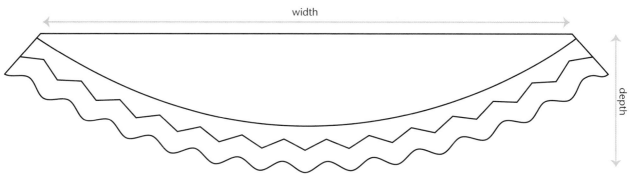

INSTRUCTIONS

1 SET UP

With gauge-size needle(s), cast on 20 sts.
Reading from the chart or written instructions,
work set-up rows 1 and 2.

2 WORK LACE

Referring to chart or written instructions, begin
lace pattern, repeating rows 1-28 a total of 15 times
to create 15 scallops. *Lace from cast-on edge should
measure 152cm / 60in.*
Rep row 1 once more. Bind off loosely.

3 PICK UP AND SHAPE HAP BODY

Examine lace; You'll see a visible line of slipped sts
along the top edge and 15 scallops / repeats along
the bottom. Place a locking stitch marker in the
slipped st on the *top* edge of the lace that marks
the end of the fifth repeat, and another at the end
of the tenth repeat. You've now marked out the
central section of your hap along which you'll pick
up sts to shape the body.

With RS facing, rejoin yarn at first marker and,
using the slipped sts along lace edge as a guide,
puk 70 sts to next marker. Remove both markers.
Turn work.
Next row (WS): K70 sts, pup 1 st, turn work. *71 sts.*
Next row (RS): K71 sts, puk 1 st, turn work. *72 sts.*

Continue as est, working back and forth in garter
st, picking up 1 stitch with every turn until you
have worked a further 60 rows. *132 sts.*

Now pick up 2 sts with each turn as foll:
Next row (WS): K132 sts, pup 2 sts, turn work.
134 sts.
Next row (RS): K134 sts, puk 2 sts, turn work.
136 sts.

Continue working back and forth in garter st as
est by last two rows until all sts are picked up and
consumed in hap body and end of lace is reached.
212 sts.

4 BIND OFF

Bind off loosely using MPSS bind-off (see special
techniques) or your preferred bind-off method.

5 FINISHING

Weave in all ends to the back of the work. Soak
hap in cool water for 20 mins. Press dry between
towels and, with blocking wires and pins, stretch
and shape to dimensions given. Leave to dry
completely.

Enjoy The Observatory!

KNIT READ WALK
THE WEST HIGHLAND WAY

All knitwear photography took place on and around the West Highland Way.

SPECIAL TECHNIQUES

A NOTE ON GAUGE AND SWATCHING

The needle sizes used in the samples are for information only - you should swatch carefully to ensure that you select the right needle size **for you** to achieve the gauge specified. It is also important to pay attention to any changes in your gauge while you are knitting, and I'd recommend double-checking your gauge when working small circumferences like sleeves, going up a needle size as necessary.

Your "gauge-size" needle is whichever size of needle gives *you* the pattern's listed gauge; for your below gauge-size needle use one size below.

A NOTE ON COLOURWORK

Strand the yarn not in use loosely along the back of the work. A "keeping pattern correct" instruction appears in the Strathendrick sweater. When this instruction appears, different sections of the pattern (such as front and back) will be divided by markers and / or steek stitches. You must keep each section separately correct. When working shaping in colourwork, remember that the direction of decreases can disrupt the continuity of the pattern if worked the "wrong" way. In the Strathendrick pattern, decreases slant *towards* the shaping lines, minimising any disruption to the pattern. Finally, steeks are *not* scary! Just refer to the series of tutorials on my website and give it a go.

REPEATING INSTRUCTIONS

Where a pattern tells you to repeat from * a certain number of times it means you should work the instruction once, and then work it a further number of times as directed. Some patterns have instructions within round brackets, and, following the brackets will tell you the number of times to work that instruction in total, or where to repeat the instructions to.

BLOCKING AND JOINING BLANKET SQUARES
youtube.com/watch?v=H7wdN2saYIM

CROCHET PROVISIONAL CAST-ON
katedaviesdesigns.com/tutorials/crochet-provisional-cast-on-tutorial/

GRAFTING
knitty.com/ISSUEsummer04/FEATtheresasum04.html

I-CORD BIND OFF
knitty.com/ISSUEfall06/FEATfall06TT.html

MPSS BIND OFF
A super stretchy simple bind off
Step A: P1.
Step B: Yo, p1. *3 sts on RH needle.*
Step C: Pass first and second sts on RH needle over third st.
Repeat steps B and C until all sts are bound off.

STEEKS
Reinforcing and cutting
katedaviesdesigns.com/2012/04/29/steeks-2-reinforcing-and-cutting/
Finishing a steek
katedaviesdesigns.com/2014/03/13/finishing-a-steek/

THREE NEEDLE BIND OFF
purlsoho.com/create/3-needle-bind-off/

TWO- COLOUR GRAFTING
katedaviesdesigns.com/tutorials/two-colour-grafting/

TURKISH OR WINDING PROVISIONAL CAST-ON
asatricosa.com/winding-cast-on/

YARN QUANTITIES
All yarn quantities are approximate and include a 5% margin for swatching and small differences in gauge / skein length.

UNITS OF MEASUREMENT
Pattern measurements have been worked in inches and then converted to centimetres using a factor of 1 in = 2.54 cm.

GLOSSARY
Bind off   UK: cast off
Stockinette   UK: stocking stitch
Gauge   UK: tension

FOR GENERAL TECHNICAL REFERENCE
June Hemmons-Hiatt	*Principles of Knitting* (2012 edn)
Margaret Radcliffe	*The Knitting Answer Book* (2006)
Montse Stanley	*The Knitter's Handbook* (2001 edn)
Elizabeth Zimmermann	*Knitting Without Tears* (1995 edn)

SUPPORT
If you have a question, please check the KDD Ravelry group where each pattern in this book has a dedicated discussion thread: **ravelry.com/groups/kate-davies-love**

If you require further assistance, please contact us by email at **info@katedaviesdesigns.com**

RESOURCES

A gallery of Tom's photographs can be found at **ootlier.com**, and his short films from the West Highland Way can be viewed on our YouTube channel: **tiny.cc/KDDyoutube**

There are numerous books and guidebooks covering the West Highland Way.
Bob Aitken and Roger Smith's official guide (Birlinn, 2016) is a good place to start, and the West Highland Way website provides a comprehensive source of up-to-date information: **westhighlandway.org**

FURTHER READING

Geoff Allan	*The Scottish Bothy Bible (2017)*
Dave Brown and Ian Mitchell	*Mountain Days and Bothy Nights (1992)*
Edmund Burt	*Letters from the North of Scotland (1754)*
Clair Calder and Lynn Lindsay	*The Islands of Loch Lomond (1992)*
Ken Crocket and Simon Richardson	*Ben Nevis: Britain's Highest Mountain (1986; 2009)*
Richard Devéria	*Duncan Bàn MacIntyre: His Life and Works (2004)*
Hamish Fraser and Irene Maver (eds)	*Glasgow: 1830 to 1912 (1995)*
Isabel Grant	*Highland Folk Ways (1995)*
Carol Kyros Walker (ed.)	*Dorothy Wordsworth: Recollections of a Tour Made in Scotland (1997)*
—— (ed.),	*Breaking Away: Coleridge in Scotland (2002)*
Edna Longley (ed.)	*Edward Thomas: The Annotated Collected Poems (2008)* "The Shieling" is reproduced here under the terms of the JISC model licence
Patrick MacGill	*Children of the Dead End: The Autobiography of a Navvy (1914)*
Ian L McHarg	*Design with Nature (1969)*
——	*To Heal the Earth: Selected Writings (1998)*
Robert Macfarlane	*The Wild Places (2007)*
Angus MacLeod (ed.)	*The Songs of Duncan Bàn MacIntyre (1952; 1978)*
Anne Macleod	*From an Antique Land: Visual Representations of the Highlands and Islands 1700–1800 (2012)*
Irene Maver	*Glasgow (2000)*
Ian R Mitchell	*Walking through Scotland's History: Two Thousand Years on Foot (2001; 2009)*
John Murray	*Reading the Gaelic Landscape (2014)*
——	*Literature of the Gaelic Landscape: Song, Poem and Tale (2017)*
Sarah Murray	*The Beauties of Scotland (1799)*
Robin Noble	*Castles in the Mist: The Victorian Transformation of the Highlands (2016)*
Michael Pollard and Tom Ang	*Walking the Scottish Highlands: General Wade's Military Roads (1984)*
RCAHMS and Historic Scotland	*The Historic Landscape of Loch Lomond and the Trossachs (2000)*
Alan Riach	*Praise of Ben Dorain (2012)*
Marjory Roy	*The Weathermen of Ben Nevis 1883–1904 (2004)*
T.C. Smout	*A History of the Scottish People, 1560–1830 (1969)*
——	*Exploring Environmental History: Selected Essays (2009; 2011)*
David Stevenson	*The Hunt for Rob Roy (2004; 2016)*
Michael A Taylor and Andrew C Kitchener	*Scotland's Beginnings (2007)*
Ian Thompson	*May the Fire Always be Lit: Biography of Jock Nimlin (1996)*
Mike Trubridge	*The Inversnaid Hotel and its Surroundings (1995)*
	Victorian Travel on the West Highland Line (1894)
Tom Weir	*Tom Weir's Scotland (1982)*
Emma Wood	*The Hydro Boys: Pioneers of Renewable Energy (2002; 2016)*

LINKS

KDD blog **katedaviesdesigns.com**

KDD shop **shopkdd.com**

 @KDDandCo

 @katedaviesdesigns

 tiny.cc/KDDyoutube

WHO MADE THIS BOOK?

Kate Davies is an author and designer. This book is her love song, through writing and knitting, to the West Highland Way, its people, and its landscape. **Tom Barr** is married to Kate and is equally at home photographing mountains or Scottish knitwear. Among her many talents, **Melanie Patton** is an extraordinary knitter who managed the organisation of this project and remained undeterred by the instruction to "knit 29 more squares." As well as editing the West Highland Way patterns, **Rachel Atkinson** is a designer and manufacturer, producing lovely woolly yarns under her *Daughter of a Shepherd* brand. **Jemima Bicknell** has an eagle eye for charts, a love of vintage style, and was this book's second technical editor. **Ivor Normand** is a copy-editor, polymath, and surprise winner of the Callanish Stones marathon in 2008. When he's not guiding visitors around Scotland's mountains, **Gordon Anderson** can be relied upon for conversation which often opens new paths of research for Kate, and was kind enough to share his spectacular Brocken spectre photographs for the chapter about Ben Nevis. **Nic Blackmore's** warm heart is in Exmoor, somewhere between her shed and her vegetable patch. Nic laid out this book and made these pages balanced and beautiful. **Claire Leach** is the generous moderator of Kate's Ravelry group and can occasionally be persuaded to model a hat. **Anna MacQuarrie** took time out from her curatorial work to check the Gaelic in Kate's account of Donnchadh Bàn. **Bruce** is a labrador retriever, and Kate and Tom's indispensable companion for countless West Highland Way walks.

CREDITS

Designs and words	Kate Davies
Photography	Tom Barr, Gordon Anderson
Project management & knitting	Melanie Patton
Editing	Rachel Atkinson, Jemima Bicknell, Ivor Normand, Anna MacQuarrie
Book design and layout	Nic Blackmore
Models	Kate Davies, Tom Barr, Melanie Patton, Claire Leach
Print & Production	Tom Barr
Canine companion	Bruce

This book is dedicated to all those who live and work on Scotland's West Highland Way.